Contents

Bertolt Brecht: 1898–1956

Brecht's life falls into three distinct phases:

From 1898 to 1933 he is in Germany.
From 1933 to 1947 during the Hitler years, he is in forced exile from Germany in various parts of the world.
In 1947 he returns to Europe, first of all to Switzerland and then to East Berlin in the German Democratic Republic (the former East Germany).

Germany

1898 Eugen Berthold Friedrich Brecht born on 10 February at Augsburg. Father employee, later director, of the Haindl paper mill.

1908 Goes to Augsburg Grammar School. Caspar Neher (later his designer) is one of his closest friends.

1913 Begins to contribute poems and essays to student newspaper.

1914 Begins to write poems, stories, reviews and essays for the literary supplement of a local newspaper. Outbreak of First World War.

1915 Caspar Neher volunteers for military service. Brecht writes to him regularly.

1916 Almost expelled for unpatriotic essay on the title: 'It is a sweet and honourable thing to die for one's country'.

1917 Enrols as medical student at Munich University. Also attends Arthur Kutscher's theatre seminar. Samples bohemian literary life of the city.

1918 Conscripted into the army and serves as a medical orderly at

Augsburg Military Hospital. Writes *Baal* and does theatre reviews for local newspaper. Becomes more involved in socialist political organisations.

1919   Writes *Drums in the Night*. Meets the comedian Karl Valentin, the theatre director Erich Engel and actresses Elisabeth Bergner, Blandine Ebinger, Carola Neher and Marianne Zoff. Brecht and Neher work to establish as many artistic and literary contacts as possible.

1920   Visits Berlin. His mother dies; he writes 'Song of my mother'.

1921   Brecht and Neher in financial difficulties. Preoccupied, Brecht fails to register for university course and is dropped from the university roll. Ends up in hospital suffering from malnutrition. New friendship with Arnolt Bronnen, a playwright, leads him to change the spelling of his name to Bertolt or Bert.

1922   Brecht summarises his life so far in a letter to Herbert Jhering on October 17:

> I first saw the light of the world in 1898. My parents hail from the Black Forest. Elementary school bored me for four years. In the nine years of my pickling at the Augsburg Realgymnasium I made no great contribution to my teachers' advancement. They never wearied of pointing out my penchant for idleness and independence. At the university I read medicine and learned to play the guitar. At secondary school I went in for all kinds of sports and developed a heart condition, which familiarised me with the secrets of metaphysics. During the war, I served as an orderly in a military hospital. After that I wrote a few plays, and in the spring of this year I was taken to the Charité hospital because of undernourishment. Arnolt Bronnen was unable to help me substantially out of his earnings as a sales clerk. After twenty-four years in the light of the world I have grown rather thin.
>
> (*Letters 1913–1956*, p. 71)

Marries Marianne Zoff in Munich. Writes *In the Jungle of the Cities*. First performance of *Drums in the Night* at the

Deutsches Theater, Berlin.

1923 Daughter, Hanne, is born. The activities of Hitler's National Socialists are hotly discussed in Brecht's Munich circle. First productions of *In the Jungle of the Cities* and *Baal* take place in Munich and Leipzig respectively. Meets Helene Weigel, the actress, for the first time.

1924 Directs Marlowe's *Edward II* which he and Lion Feuchtwanger – celebrated novelist and playwright as well as being dramatic adviser to the Kammerspiele in Munich – had adapted. Brecht was already using certain devices (plot summaries before scenes, white face make-up to indicate fear) to induce critical detachment in actors and audience. Finally settles in Berlin. Is taken on as dramaturg (literary adviser) at Max Reinhardt's Deutsches Theater. Helene Weigel bears him a son, Stefan. Meets Elisabeth Hauptmann who becomes his constant collaborator.

1925 Writes poems, visits Marianne Zoff and Hanne. Congratulates G.B. Shaw on his seventieth birthday, commending his 'keen intelligence and fearless eloquence'. Completes manuscript of *Man equals Man* which he presents to Elisabeth Hauptmann as thanks for her unstinting and unpaid work. Joins 'Group 25', aiming to co-ordinate the interests of younger authors not represented by literary groups dominated by the older generation.

1926 *Man equals Man* premiered at Darmstadt and Düsseldorf. Works on a play (never finished) called *Joe Fleischhacker*, which was to deal with the Chicago Wheat Exchange; leads him to the study of Marx as the only adequate method of analysing the workings of capitalism.

1927 Divorces Marianne Zoff. Works with Erwin Piscator, the pioneer of communist political theatre in Germany, on a dramatisation of Hašek's novel, *The Good Soldier Schweik*. First collaboration with Kurt Weill, on *Mahagonny* – with Lotte

Lenya and designs by Neher.

1928   *The Threepenny Opera*, music by Kurt Weill, words by Brecht
(based on a translation of John Gay's *Beggar's Opera* by
Elisabeth Hauptmann), opens at Theater am Schiffbauerdamm –
hit of the season. Brecht had transferred bourgeois manners to a
Soho criminal setting.

1929   Marries Helene Weigel. *The Baden-Baden Cantata* staged at
Baden-Baden Music Festival, music by Hindemith. The Brecht/
Weill *Berlin Requiem* broadcast on the radio. Premiere of
Hauptmann/Brecht/Weill musical *Happy End*.

1930   Daughter Barbara born. His *Lehrstück* or didactic play, *The
Measures Taken*, with music by Hanns Eisler, is given its first
performance in Berlin. The communist didactic plays for
amateur performance were intended to clarify the ideas of the
performers as much as the audience. The first performance of
The Rise and Fall of the City of Mahagonny, an opera with
words by Brecht and music by Kurt Weill, causes a riot as the
Nazis voice their criticism at Leipzig. In his notes on the opera,
Brecht lists the differences between the traditional *dramatic* (or
Aristotelian) and the new *epic* (or non-Aristotelian) theatre at
which he is aiming. The *Lehrstücke, He Said Yes/He Said No* –
two 'school operas' by Brecht and Weill – staged by schoolboys
and an amateur orchestra in Berlin.

1931   Completes *St Joan of the Stockyards* – not performed until 1959.
The G.W. Pabst film version of *The Threepenny Opera* opens in
Berlin following a lawsuit to prevent it, which Brecht loses.

1932   Brecht's only film *Kühle Wampe* held up by the censor. His
dramatisation of Maxim Gorky's novel *The Mother* is
performed by left-wing collective in Berlin, music by Hanns
Eisler, and demonstrates development of a worker's mother
towards proletarian class-consciousness. Beginning of friendship
with Margarete Steffin. Studies Marxism under dissident
communist Karl Korsch.

Exile

1933 Nazis come to power. The night after the German parliament building (the Reichstag) is burnt down, Brecht flees with his family to Prague. Moves to Vienna, then Zurich, finally settling on the island of Fyn in Denmark. Friendship with Ruth Berlau begins. Premiere of the Brecht/Weill *The Seven Deadly Sins* in Paris with Lotte Lenya and choreography by George Balanchine.

1934 Writes *The Threepenny Novel*, a more obviously Marxist version of *The Threepenny Opera*. Redrafts, with Hanns Eisler and Margarete Steffin, *Round Heads and Pointed Heads or Empires of a Feather Flock Together. An atrocity fairy tale.* Walter Benjamin stays with Brecht. Visits London. Themes of flight and exile enter his poems. Helene Weigel and children in Vienna and Zurich.

1935 Visits Moscow, talks to Soviet dramatist Sergei Tretiakov about the 'alienation effect'. Attends International Writers' Conference in Paris. Brecht is stripped of his German citizenship by the Nazis. Visits New York to look in on a production of *The Mother* which does not meet with his approval. Negotiates American edition of *The Threepenny Novel* and a performance of *Round Heads*.

1936 Attends International Writers' Conference in London. Lives in Hampstead. Writes anti-fascist poetry. Consultant on first production of *Round Heads* in Danish in the Riddersalen in Copenhagen.

1937 Completes the Spanish play *Señora Carrar's Rifles*. Writes children's songs for Helene Weigel. Attends International Writers' Conference in Paris: main theme, intellectuals' attitudes towards the Spanish Civil War. Brands self 'one of the cowards' for being too cautious to go to Madrid himself. In Paris, a performance of *The Threepenny Opera* and the world premiere of *Señora Carrar's Rifles* (with Helene Weigel, 'dedicated to the heroic fight for freedom of the Spanish people'). Calls Helene Weigel's acting 'the best and the purest that could be seen so far in the epic theatre anywhere'.

1938 Franco's right-wing Falangists emerge as the likely victors in the Spanish Civil War and Chamberlain signs away the Sudetenland in the Munich Treaty in an effort to appease Hitler. The growing power of fascism, developments in the Soviet Union, his steadily diminishing chances of seeing his plays performed anywhere and the ensuing money worries increase his sense of isolation. On Easter Sunday writes the poem 'Spring 1938':

> In the willows by the sound
> These spring nights the screech-owl often calls.
> According to a peasant superstition
> Your screech-owl informs people that
> They haven't long to live. I
> Who know full well that I told the truth
> About the powers that be, don't need a death-bird
> To inform me so.
>
> (trans. Derek Bowman, *Poems 1913–1956*, Methuen, p. 304)

Fear and Misery in the Third Reich premiered in Paris. Writes *Life of Galileo*, assisted by Margarete Steffin. In December, news of fission of uranium by physicists Hahn and Strassmann causes revisions to text.

1939 Hitler annexes Czechoslovakia. Works by Brecht confiscated and pulped. Moves to Stockholm with his family. Finishes *Mother Courage and her Children*. Not allowed to participate in political activities but continues under pseudonym of John Kent. Father dies and is buried in Augsburg. Works on *The Good Person of Szechwan*. Soviet Union invades Finland.

1940 German forces march into Denmark and Norway. Moves with family to Helsinki, expressing gratitude for help and friendship he found in Stockholm:

> It's a big thing to find so much intellectual solidarity even (and especially) in these dark times . . . I had the feeling that I was leaving my home.
>
> (Letter to Henry Peter Matthis, *Letters 1913–1956*, p. 323)

Drafts *Mr Puntila and his Man Matti*, works with Hella Wuolijoki. Severe food shortage. Waits for visas to go to America.

1941   Completes *The Good Person of Szechwan*, *Mr Puntila and his Man Matti* and *The Resistible Rise of Arturo Ui*, the last in collaboration with Margarete Steffin. Writes war poetry and 'Finnish Epigrams'. Travels through the Soviet Union via Leningrad and Moscow to Vladivostock and sails to the USA. Greatly affected by death of Margarete Steffin from pneumonia in a Moscow hospital:

> In Year Nine of the flight from Hitler
> Exhausted by travelling
> By cold and by hunger in wintry Finland
> And by waiting for a passport to another continent
> Our comrade Steffin died
> In the red city of Moscow.
>
> ('After the death of my collaborator M.S.', trans. John Willett, *Poems 1913–1956*, p. 364)

Arrives in Los Angeles in July, settles in Santa Monica. Makes contact with other European exiles, e.g. Heinrich Mann, Lion Feuchtwanger and Fritz Lang, and also with Americans such as Orson Welles and Eric Bentley. First performance of *Mother Courage and her Children* in neutral Switzerland.

1942   Prepares *Poems in Exile* for publication. Participates in anti-war, anti-fascist activities of exile groups. Meets Charles Laughton. Finds it difficult to adjust to American values: 'but all that stands there as if it were in a showcase, and I involuntarily search every mountain and every lemon tree for a small price tag.' Registered as both subject to military service and as an 'enemy alien'.

1943   First performances of *The Good Person of Szechwan* and *Life of Galileo* in Zurich. Mussolini resigns. Brecht caught in extended argument with Thomas Mann about the differences between Germany and Hitler.

1944   Brecht becomes member of newly formed Council for a Democratic Germany. Finishes first version of *The Caucasian Chalk Circle*. Studies Arthur Waley's translations of Chinese poetry. Begins to revise *Galileo* with Charles Laughton.

1945   *Fear and Misery in the Third Reich* performed in New York under title of *The Private Life of the Master Race*. English version of *Galileo* further revised after dropping of atomic bombs on Hiroshima and Nagasaki, to stress the social responsibility of the scientist.

1946   First performance of Brecht's adaptation of Webster's *The Duchess of Malfi* in Boston.

1947   Charles Laughton appears in the title role of *Galileo* in Beverly Hills and New York. Brecht appears before the 'House Committee on Un-American Activities', proves himself master of ambiguity when cross-examined about his communist sympathies.

Return

Brecht and Helene Weigel go to Zurich, leaving son, Stefan, an American citizen, in USA. Meets up again with Caspar Neher as well as playwrights, Max Frisch and Carl Zuckmayer. First applies for Austrian passport (Weigel is Austrian).

1948   Adaptation of Sophocles' *Antigone* performed in Chur, Switzerland. *Mr Puntila and his Man Matti* premiered in Zurich. Publishes *Little Organum for the Theatre*. Travels to Berlin, starts rehearsals for *Mother Courage* at Deutsches Theater in Soviet sector of city. *The Caucasian Chalk Circle* first performed in Eric and Maja Bentley's English translation by students at Northfield, Minnesota.

1949   *Mother Courage* opens at Deutsches Theater with Helene
        Weigel in title role. Brecht visits Zurich again before settling in
        Berlin. The Berliner Ensemble, Brecht and Weigel's own state-
        subsidised company, is formed and opens with *Puntila*. Brecht
        applies again for Austrian passport.

1951   *The Mother* is performed by the Berliner Ensemble. Brecht
        finishes first version of adaptation of Shakespeare's *Coriolanus*.

1953   When Stalin dies in April, Brecht writes:

> The oppressed people of five continents, those who have already
> liberated themselves, and all those who are fighting for world peace,
> must have felt their hearts miss a beat when they heard that Stalin
> was dead. He was the embodiment of their hopes. But the intellectual
> and material weapons which he produced remain, and with them the
> method to produce new ones.
>
> (*Brecht on Art and Politics*, Methuen, 2002)

Brecht elected President of the German section of the PEN
Club, the international writers' association. On 17 June there are
strikes and demonstrations protesting about working conditions
in the German Democratic Republic. Brecht angry that a
doctored version of a letter he wrote is published, making it
seem that he sympathised with the forcible suppression of the
workers' uprising.

1954   Berliner Ensemble acquires its own home at Theater am
        Schiffbauerdamm. German premiere of *The Caucasian Chalk
        Circle* but 'The Struggle for the Valley' is omitted as being
        politically inopportune. Brecht makes public his objections to
        the Paris Treaty (which incorporated the Federal Republic of
        Germany into Nato) and to re-armament in general. Brecht in
        Bruges, Amsterdam and Paris where Berliner Ensemble gives
        performances of *Mother Courage* and Kleist's *The Broken
        Pitcher*. Productions greeted with great acclaim at the Paris
        Théâtre des Nations festival. Brecht awarded Stalin Peace Prize.

1955   Travels to Moscow to receive Stalin Peace Prize. In his acceptance speech he explains how his thinking has been shaped by particular writings and events:

> The most important lesson was that a future for mankind was becoming visible only 'from below', from the standpoint of the oppressed and exploited. Only by fighting with them does one fight for mankind.
>
> (*Brecht on Art and Politics*)

By the end of the year suffering from exhaustion and unwell.

1956   Travels to Milan to attend final rehearsals and first night of Giorgio Strehler's production of *The Threepenny Opera*. Brecht's health prevents him from carrying on rehearsing, preparing Berliner Ensemble, now recognised as foremost progressive theatre in Europe, for a visit to London. Hands over direction to Erich Engel. 14 August Brecht dies of a heart attack. Berliner Ensemble visit to London goes ahead very successfully. At the official memorial celebration of Brecht's life, his own version of his epitaph is quoted:

> I need no gravestone, but
> If you need one for me
> I would like it to bear these words:
> He made suggestions. We
> Carried them out.
> Such an inscription would
> Honour us all.
>
> (trans. Michael Hamburger, *Poems 1913–1956*, p. 218)

1965   Second visit of the Berliner Ensemble to London with three new productions plus a revival of *The Threepenny Opera* directed by Erich Engel.

Plot

Prologue

The scene is a fair in the Soho region of London. A ballad singer
sings 'The Ballad of Mac the Knife', during the course of which
the Peachum family are seen to cross the stage. At the end of the
song, Macheath, whose nefarious exploits have been the subject of
the ballad, emerges from among a group of whores, is identified by
one of them, then exits.

Act One

Scene One: In his outfitting shop for beggars Peachum sings his
'Morning Hymn', the sentiments of which smack of the hell-fire
sermon: Christians, get on with your sinful employment,
God's Judgement is far from a joke. He then complains that
business isn't good because people become too accustomed to pious
biblical phrases and give less and less to beggars on the street
bearing placards with these phrases designed to soften the meanest
of hearts. It emerges that his business is trading in misery and
guilt. He has divided London into fourteen districts and, for a
sizeable fee and a percentage of the earnings, licenses beggars to
ply their trade in a particular area. His emporium is also a
theatrical outfitters in that he supplies the beggars with costumes
and properties designed not to horrify but to elicit sympathy from
passers-by. The tattered garments, which have been specially made
with false dirt stains ironed into them, are designed to make the
external trappings of misery and disability aesthetically tolerable, if
not exactly pleasing, and therefore approachable. Human suffering,

injury and neglect must never appear too real, for fear of putting off potential donors. Therefore, each beggar needs to be a performer in order to portray suffering artistically rather than be a living embodiment of distress. Independent beggars are beaten up by Peachum's employees and forced to join the equivalent of a beggars' trade union. Such a one is Filch, who appears at Peachum's shop, pays his fee, and is assigned a costume and a district. At this point we learn from Mrs Peachum that their daughter, Polly, has been seeing 'a fine gentleman', whom Peachum recognises to be the notorious Mac the Knife. They are then horrified to discover that Polly's bed has not been slept in the previous night. The scene concludes with 'The "No They Can't" Song', in which the Peachums warn against the dangers of romantic love and deplore the fact that people like their daughter go out pleasure-seeking instead of staying quietly at home.

Scene Two: It is five in the afternoon and the scene is a bare stable owned by the Duke of Devonshire which, during the course of the action, will be transformed into a Victorian living room for the celebration of Macheath and Polly's wedding. An assortment of furniture of various historical periods has been especially stolen for the occasion by members of Macheath's gang. The scene parodies the civilities of a wedding reception, here interspersed with descriptions of the violence meted out in order to arrange it. Mac, a violent criminal, spends a good deal of the scene incongruously schooling his gang in points of polite etiquette. Four members of the gang sing a song about a wedding for poor people who feel compelled to go through the motions of acquiring a degree of married respectability. This is followed by Polly's singing a song about Pirate Jenny, a girl who has been insulted and humiliated sexually and socially and who fantasises in a frighteningly destructive manner about the revenge she will wreak on society and the male of the species in particular. The gang then panic when the arrival of the police is announced in the person of the High Sheriff, Tiger Brown. The gang are next surprised and relieved to learn that Macheath and Tiger Brown are old pals from their army days and that Brown knows all about Mac's criminal activities, in which he has a profitable share and to which he turns a blind eye. Together they sing 'The Cannon Song', which presents a highly critical description of an army which sees its recruits as anonymous cannon-fodder and a colonialism characterised by racial violence. The gang then unveil a bed which converts the stable into a boudoir where Mac and Polly are to spend the first night of their honeymoon. The scene ends with a love song between them.

Scene Three: The scene reverts to Peachum's Outfitting Emporium for Beggars where the Peachums have been made aware of Polly's marriage. They have previously expressed fear that she will inadvertently betray their criminal activities to Macheath, a business competitor, who will inform the police, and now they deplore her throwing herself away when she could have proved a lucrative marriage investment. Polly sings a song in explanation of her behaviour, which suggests that she grew tired of giving the brush-off to respectable wooers whom she could sexually manipulate, but was powerless to resist someone who was not respectable and who swept her off her feet. Five beggars arrive, one of whom complains about the quality of the leg-stump provided him. Peachum makes adjustments to, and comments on, the beggars' appearance and emphasises that successful begging is an art form. The Peachums then turn their attention to Polly, suggesting first that she divorce Macheath. Mrs Peachum insists that he is a well-known philanderer who has, no doubt, already fathered several illegitimate children. Polly leaves and they discuss the possibility of handing Macheath over to the police and claiming the £40 reward, little suspecting that Tiger Brown is his friend. Polly, who has overheard them, warns against trying to impeach Macheath as there is nothing on record against him at Scotland Yard. Peachum is nevertheless determined that Mac the Knife will hang by the end of the week. All three then sing the First Threepenny Finale, 'Concerning the Insecurity of the Human Condition', the theme of which is that human beings would improve their own condition if they could, aim for higher things and do what the Bible exhorts them to do, were it not for the fact that all striving is pointless because the world is a harsh and wicked place and mankind is fundamentally irredeemable.

Act Two
Scene Four: Polly returns to the stable and warns Mac that her father has been to see Brown and, whereas formerly there was nothing on record against him, there is now a whole list of charges, including attempted murder, which she reads out. However, none of this seems to diminish her ardour for him in any way. She advises him to make his getaway and Mac leaves her instructions with regard to managing the gang and handling its finances. We also learn that the Coronation celebrations, which are about to begin, are the reason for Brown's about-face on the question of Macheath's criminal record. Peachum is blackmailing Brown by threatening to get his beggars to disrupt the Coronation procession and disgrace Brown in the eyes of his superiors and the newly-crowned queen. The gang arrive and Macheath places Polly in charge of them – something which they initially resent, but applaud when they realise she can be as domineering as any man. Reassuring each other of their undying devotion, Macheath and Polly act out a sentimentally romantic scene before taking leave of each other. In an Interlude before the next scene, it becomes clear that Mrs Peachum has anticipated that Macheath will visit his brothel as usual and has bribed Jenny to turn him in to the police when he next visits her. She sings 'The Ballad of Sexual Obsession', to the effect that whether hero, genius, religious convert or would-

be rebel, all are destined to succumb to and be compromised by basic animal instinct.

Scene Five: Mrs Peachum is right. The sexual instinct has proved more powerful than the instinct for flight and Macheath, instead of heading for the open road, has ended up at his usual Thursday night brothel which, instead of being a seedy place, turns out to be a 'bourgeois idyll'. Jake, one of the gang, is also there but seems more interested in reading the newspaper than fraternisation. Mac chats with the girls and Jenny reads his fortune, giving him a hint – which he ignores – of her treachery. She then slips out to get the police, and is joined by Mrs Peachum. They stand under a streetlight with Constable Smith while Mac, inside, sings the 'Ballad of Immoral Earnings', which Jenny joins in. In quasi-romantic fashion they recall the days when Mac played pimp to Jenny's whore, beat her up when he felt like it, slept with her in the afternoons, and disposed of any unwanted offspring in the city sewer. They begin a dance but are interrupted by Constable Smith who tries to arrest Mac. The latter attempts to escape through a window but jumps straight into the arms of the law.

Scene Six: The scene moves to a police cell where Brown is hoping and praying that Mac has managed to escape. He seems more concerned with fear of seeming disloyal to Macheath than in seeking the means to pacify Peachum. At this point Macheath is brought in and looks at Brown with 'a withering glance'; Brown breaks down in tears. Mac then bribes Constable Smith with a cheque for fifty guineas for a lighter pair of handcuffs and sings the 'Ballad of Good Living', which suggests that those who see the point of existence on this planet as anything other than having a good time and acquiring a lot of money are both foolish and misguided. Tiger Brown's daughter, Lucy, then enters and confronts Macheath. As far as she is concerned, Macheath is betrothed to her, but she has discovered that he has married Polly. Mac denies it and promises to marry Lucy. At this point Polly enters and Mac finds himself an object of dispute between the two women who, instead of ganging up against him, sing a 'Jealousy Duet' in which each vies with the other for prior claim to his affections. The sung quarrel then continues as a spoken dispute until Mrs Peachum arrives and drags Polly away. Mac takes this opportunity to make up to Lucy and persuades her to hand him his hat and swordstick through the cell bars before she leaves. Smith enters the cell to retrieve the swordstick and Mac seizes the chance to escape. When Peachum arrives to collect his reward from Brown the bird has flown and Peachum, who believes that Brown has contrived Mac's escape, threatens disruption of the Coronation procession and the humiliation of the police chief. The Second Threepenny Finale, 'What Keeps Mankind Alive', is sung by Mac, Jenny and an offstage chorus. Its theme is that it is only by being bestial and behaving as if one were not a human being that mankind manages to survive at all.

Act Three
Scene Seven: The scene shifts to Peachum's Emporium where a group of beggars is getting ready to disrupt the Coronation, aided it would seem by another 1,432 offstage beggar employees. The whores arrive to claim their reward from Mrs Peachum for turning Macheath over to the law but, as he has managed to escape, she refuses to hand over the money. Jenny then launches into a defence of the man who has exploited and abused her but inadvertently reveals that he's now with Suky Tawdry. Mrs Peachum sings another verse of the 'Ballad of Sexual Obsession'. Peachum gives the order for the beggars to march on Buckingham Palace but they are thwarted by the arrival of Tiger Brown bent on arresting them before they have the chance to cause a disturbance. Peachum and

Brown face up to each other before Peachum sings 'The Song of the Insufficiency of Human Endeavour', which proposes the idea that mankind is never sharp, bad, or undemanding enough for this 'bleak existence'. The fact that mankind continues to declaim its erroneous faith in its own humanity is a pathetically worthy trait but is, ultimately, a waste of time and energy. Peachum then points out to Brown that, although the police chief can arrest those beggars present, he cannot possibly arrest the other thousand or so currently bearing down on the Coronation through the streets of London. Next, having just defended Macheath against Peachum's insults, Jenny now betrays him once more by telling Brown the address in Oxford Street where he is currently 'consoling' Suky Tawdry. Brown sets out to arrest him again, with Peachum's demand ringing in his ears that Macheath be hanged by 6 a.m. Peachum then sings the final verse of 'The Song of the Insufficiency of Human Endeavour', which suggests that the only way to ensure that man behaves decently is to slug him 'good and dead'. The scene concludes with the 'Solomon Song', sung by Jenny which advises against qualities such as wisdom, beauty, courage, curiosity and passion which, admirable though they may be in principle, only cause the deaths of their possessors and so become a curse rather than a blessing.

Scene Eight: The setting is Lucy's room at the Old Bailey to which Polly has come, ostensibly to make amends for their earlier quarrel but, in actual fact, to discover exactly what Lucy's relationship with Macheath amounts to and where he is at the moment. The complex scene runs a gamut of differing moods and emotions as Polly and Lucy try to outmanoeuvre each other in claiming their rights to Macheath as if he were a piece of property, before striking up a feminist bargain against him. Their true feelings about Macheath are revealed when Polly collapses when news is brought that he has been arrested again. She is revived by Mrs Peachum who tells her she will make a lovely widow if she cheers up and makes her change into a mourning outfit ready for the hanging.

Scene Nine: The final scene takes place in the death cell and occupies the hour between 5 and 6 a.m. on the Friday when Macheath is due to be hanged. The scene makes us aware of the passing of time as the minutes tick away, prompting Macheath to sing his 'Call from the Grave', which conveys his agitated state as he contemplates his own extinction. Two members of his gang arrive, whom Mac urges to obtain the money which Constable Smith has hinted might gain his release. They leave to draw out their savings of £400 but Smith rejects this as insufficient. While the gallows is being prepared in the background, Macheath sings the second verse of his 'Call from the Grave', before Polly enters and conducts a very self-possessed conversation with her husband before breaking down. As she exits, Smith and Tiger Brown bring Macheath his last meal, a dish of asparagus, which he has requested. Macheath and Brown then go over the financial accounts for the previous six months of their criminal relationship. Brown becomes emotional before flouncing out in high dudgeon claiming his honour has been insulted, but Macheath seems concerned that feelings should not get in the way of business transactions, even on the brink of eternity. Smith returns and, because the bribe money has not been raised, announces that the deal is off. During his last minutes on earth, a queue of people is admitted to see Macheath. They file past his cell: Polly, Lucy, the whores, Parson Kimball, two members of the gang, Peachum, who is setting eyes on his son-in-law for the first time, Mrs Peachum and Brown. Mac is let out of his cell and delivers a speech in which he adopts the persona of a lower-middle class artisan whose fate has been determined by the more powerful forces of corporate capitalism, plus a sequence of 'unfortunate circumstances'. He then sings the 'Ballad in Which Macheath Begs All Men For Forgiveness'. The plea for forgiveness for his own and others' sins is even extended, reluctantly, to the police.

The procession to the gallows follows but, at the point where Macheath is standing beneath the rope waiting for the drop, Peachum calls a halt to the proceedings by reminding everyone that this is an opera and, like the beggar in Gay's original, contrives a happy ending. This takes the form of Tiger Brown's arrival on horseback to announce that Macheath has received a royal pardon, has also been elevated to the peerage and awarded a sizeable pension for life. The opera concludes with general rejoicing but also with a cynical chorus which advocates that injustice should not be resisted but allowed to freeze to death of its own accord in a world which, by its very nature, is harsh and cold and full of our miserable cries. The bells of Westminster Abbey, celebrating the Coronation, ring out for a third time as if in ironic celebration of this final sentiment.

Commentary

Who was Bertolt Brecht?

Throughout his life Brecht challenged accepted conventions and attitudes, in his personal, political and theatrical lives. He is one of the seminal figures in twentieth-century theatre and yet remains a problematic character because there are so many contradictions evident in his actions and pronouncements. It seems impossible to pin him down absolutely – just when you think you know exactly what he intends, you will find a conflicting element.

When Brecht died, shortly before midnight on 14 August 1956 in his flat in East Berlin, he was a world-famous playwright and director. He was an extremely important figure in the new German Democratic Republic (GDR), the communist state that had been established in the Soviet occupation zone of Germany in October 1949 and was dissolved in October 1990. Brecht had thought very carefully about how he wanted to be buried. He chose, within a graveyard near to his own flat, a grave a few metres away from that of the philosopher Hegel, the father of 'dialectics' – the view of discourse in terms of thesis/antithesis and their interaction, which provided the philosophical underpinnings for Marxism and was also central to Brecht's literary work. The day after a private funeral attended only by family, close friends and colleagues, came the official state ceremony, at which the GDR's most important political and cultural figures almost queued up to pay tribute to Brecht.

This would have delighted Brecht who had always carefully courted publicity and cultivated his image. Equally he had cast himself as being 'different' from everybody else in the ways he sought to impress those who could give him access to the literary scene. The novelist, Lion

Feuchtwanger, recalled the impact of his first meeting with Brecht:

> He was slight, badly shaved, shabbily dressed. He stayed close to the walls, spoke with a Swabian accent, had written a play, was called Bertolt Brecht. The play was entitled *Spartacus*.
>
> Most young authors presenting a manuscript point out that they have torn this work from their bleeding hearts: but this young man emphasised that he had written *Spartacus* purely in order to make money.
>
> (*Brecht: As They Knew Him*, ed. Hubert Witt, trans. John Peet, Lawrence and Wishart, London, 1975, p. 17)

This play, which Brecht renamed at Feuchtwanger's suggestion *Drums in the Night*, provided Brecht's breakthrough into the literary world. It won Brecht the coveted Kleist Prize, making him one of the most widely known literary figures in Germany at the time (1922) and effectively launching his career, which would span the next three and a half decades.

Throughout his adult life Brecht maintained a strong conviction of his own genius. He was determined to keep control over the ways his plays were performed, largely because he was convinced that most theatre directors had no understanding of what he was trying to accomplish. The ways in which he interfered in stage productions, which frequently involved hurling insults at actors and directors, did not always win him friends. But ultimately his insistence on doing things his way or not at all usually paid off.

Important figures in Brecht's life
His collaborators: Brecht liked to work collectively and throughout most of his professional life he collaborated with a succession of women who typed his manuscripts, helped him to develop his ideas and contributed to the writing of his plays. Before 1933 this role fell to Elisabeth Hauptmann, who edited Brecht's *Collected Works* after his death. During his years in exile in Scandinavia, his closest companion

was Margarete Steffin who worked with Brecht on the manuscripts of his finest plays, such as *Life of Galileo* and *Mother Courage and her Children*. 'Grete' Steffin's death from tuberculosis in 1941 in Moscow on the journey from Finland to the United States affected Brecht very deeply. Her place was taken by Ruth Berlau who went to the States with Brecht and also returned to post-war Berlin with him. These three women served Brecht with remarkable devotion – a devotion not always reciprocated. Without them, particularly Margarete Steffin, some of his greatest work might not have been written.

His composers: From the outset Brecht's songs became an essential component of his plays. At first he composed the tunes himself but then he began working with professional musicians. He worked principally with three composers: Kurt Weill for six years (1927–33), Hanns Eisler for two lengthy periods, separated by Eisler's departure to the USA (1929–38, 1949–56), and Paul Dessau for the last phase of his life (1946–56). Whilst working with Weill and Eisler, up to 1938, Brecht and the composers were true collaborators, with the musical component of plays such as *Happy End* and *The Threepenny Opera* being integral to the text, giving a distinctive sound and flavour to the productions. However, although Brecht retained close contact with Eisler during his own exile in America, they did not work closely together from 1938 onwards. The plays written during this time were written without any integral musical component. Brecht's working arrangements with Eisler and Dessau from 1946 were not at the same collaborative level; from 1936 to the end of his life, no Brecht play bears a composer's name among the 'collaborators' listed after its title.

His wife: Helene Weigel, Brecht's second wife, held the most important place in his life. She was not involved in the writing of his plays but many of his parts were written with her in mind and her acting influenced the ways in which Brecht conceived of his plays on stage. Throughout the years of exile and when they returned to Germany, Weigel managed the Brecht household – a difficult task given the constant stream of visitors and the journeying from one country to another. After Brecht's death, Weigel ran the Berliner Ensemble theatre. She died in 1971.

Stage designer: Caspar Neher, Brecht's boyhood friend, became a celebrated stage designer whose often stark, innovative sets have become a hallmark of Brechtian theatre. He designed sets for productions of *In the Jungle of the Cities* (1923), *Edward II* (1924), *Baal* (1926) and *The Threepenny Opera* (1928), among others. His settings used gradations of subdued colours and brilliant stage lighting in the spirit of the play being performed. In 1948 after the war, he rejoined forces with Brecht, designing the set for *Antigone* in Switzerland. He designed *Mr Puntila and his Man Matti* (1949) and *Life of Galileo* in 1957 for the Berliner Ensemble.

It is important to realise that Brecht did not regard his written manuscript as the finished product. What counted was what was performed on stage. Brecht was a compulsive reviser. He was always willing to alter his plays when he saw how they worked on stage. Therefore the influence of Weigel and Neher, in particular, was not a matter of a few afterthoughts but a central part of Brecht's methods of production.

Brecht's politics

Born into a well-to-do bourgeois family in the Bavarian city of Augsburg, Brecht lived through two world wars, the rise and fall of the most murderous and brutal dictatorship, and the division of his country – a historical context that framed his phenomenal literary output. During the First World War Brecht became a medical student at the University of Munich and then, from October 1918 to January 1919, served as an orderly at a clinic for soldiers with venereal disease. He witnessed the revolutionary upheavals of early 1919 in Munich but was more interested in the theatre and women. He seems to have played no coherent political role at all, more concerned with being an angry young man out to shock respectable bourgeois society.

During the early 1920s he was greatly influenced by Expressionism and the experimental theatre of the time. However, in 1926, Brecht, while researching material for a play about the Chicago grain exchange, discovered the writings of Karl Marx and the theory of dialectics. The play was never completed but in Marx Brecht found what he regarded as the key to understanding the world around him and to the historical process, as well as a framework and structure for his own writing. Brecht's work became didactic, seeking to teach and encourage active thought by the audience. For Brecht, the task became the tearing away of surface appearances to expose the true nature of society.

Despite his commitment to Marxist ideology and the explicitly left-wing nature of many of his plays, Brecht never joined the Communist Party. At the same time the success of his plays made him famous and earned him a good living. During his exile from Germany he lived comfortably despite his unsuccessful attempts to sell scripts in Hollywood or to get his plays performed in New York. During his time in the USA he was hauled before the House Committee on Un-American Activities and accused of being a member of the Communist Party. Brecht proved himself a master of ambiguity and political survival with his cleverly crafted replies. When he returned to his native land, he did settle in the Soviet Communist sector of East Berlin but perhaps a major attraction was that he was given a theatre there. It is interesting to note that after his return to Berlin, Brecht did not write any more plays – he concentrated on putting into practice a new style of theatre.

Even when he lived in a state which officially sanctioned Marxism, Brecht remained a controversial figure, since his style of epic theatre was at odds with the official Stalinist line of Socialist Realism. Brecht ensured that he kept his options open by having an Austrian passport which allowed him to travel freely in the West and he also maintained his contacts with his West German publisher, Peter Suhrkamp.

In June 1953 there was an uprising of workers against the GDR government. Brecht did not openly support either side, although the content of his plays would perhaps lead us to expect that he would have supported the workers. Instead he adopted a critical and ambiguous stance of solidarity with the government. He wrote a letter to the party leader in which he affirmed his loyal allegiance to the Socialist Unity Party but then afterwards wrote a sharply satirical poem in which he attacked the actions of the GDR. It seemed impossible to pin down exactly where Brecht's loyalties lay. Equally confusing, given Brecht's intense opposition to fascism, was his failure to voice any criticism of the Stalinist regime in the USSR (and GDR). He alienated many in the West by his acceptance of the Stalin Peace Prize in 1955.

Brecht's views on theatre

Brecht came to public notice as an opponent of the then fashionable theatre of illusion as characterised by the work of Max Reinhardt and Konstantin Stanislavsky, but he was also opposed to the expressionist approach which emphasised overt, declamatory demonstrations of feelings. He drew up a rough-and-ready yet basic distinction between the old Aristotelian theatre, which he generally called 'dramatic' and associated with the social dramas of Ibsen, and his own new theatre which he called 'epic' and on which his theories and practice – especially with his own company the Berliner Ensemble – were based. From the beginning of his career Brecht had fought a running battle against the conventional theatre of his day, labelling it as 'culinary' because, like good cooking, it satisfied the senses but did not engage the mind. For the production of one of his first plays, *Drums in the Night* in 1922, he had banners put up in the auditorium telling the audience not to 'gawp so romantically' and in his essay in 1935, 'On Experimental Theatre', Brecht asked:

> How can the theatre be entertaining and at the same time instructive? How can it be taken out of the traffic in intellectual drugs and transformed from a place of illusion to a place of insight?

For Brecht the traditional or dramatic theatre was a place where the audience was absorbed into a comforting illusion which played on its emotions and left its members drained, but with a sense of satisfaction which predisposed them to accept the world as it was. What he himself was looking for was a theatre that would help to change the world.

The term 'epic' was in use in German debates before Brecht adapted it, and he drew on several sources in generating his own interpretation:

> the political theatre of Erwin Piscator and German agitprop; the cabaret of Frank Wedekind and the work of the music hall comedian Karl Valentin; Charlie Chaplin and the American silent film; Asian and revolutionary Soviet theatre; as well as Shakespeare and Elizabethan chronicle plays.
>
> (Peter Brooker, 'Key Words in Brecht's Theory and Practice' in *The Cambridge Companion to Brecht*, ed. Thomson and Sacks, Cambridge, 1994)

He first set out his ideas on epic theatre in his 'Notes on the Opera *The Rise and Fall of the City of Mahagonny*', where he listed the main characteristics of 'dramatic' and 'epic' theatre, insisting, however, that the contrasts he was highlighting were not absolute but rather a matter of emphasis. Although the following table gives a good starting point for a consideration of Brecht's theory and practice, it should be noted that Brecht in conducting his campaign to change the dominant mode of theatre, tended at this point to overstress the differences, for example the contrast between 'feeling' and 'reason' he never took to be absolute. He knew perfectly well that plenty of 'dramatic' plays arouse thought and that in his own 'epic' plays feeling was by no means excluded. It is therefore important to recognise the element of tactical exaggeration in the way he presents his table of differences.

Dramatic theatre	Epic theatre
plot	narrative
implicates the spectator in a stage situation	turns the spectator into an observer but
wears down the capacity for action	arouses the capacity for action
provides sensations	forces decisions
experience	picture of the world
the spectator is involved in something	is made to face something
suggestion	argument
instinctive feelings are preserved	brought to the point of recognition
the spectator is in the thick of it, shares the experience	the spectator stands outside, studies
the human being is taken for granted	the human being is the object of the enquiry
the human being is unalterable	is alterable and able to alter
eyes on the finish	eyes on the course
one scene makes another	each scene for itself
growth	montage
linear development	in curves
evolutionary determinism	jumps
the human being as a fixed point	the human being as a process
thought determines being	social being determines thought
feeling	reason

(*Brecht on Theatre*, p. 37, with slight modifications)

In drawing up this list Brecht challenged traditional ways of

classifying texts. The term 'dramatic' is usually associated with
texts written for performance where the characters and settings
represented in the writing are limited by the conventions and
resources of the theatre. The length of a piece of dramatic writing
is also limited by the audience's patience and concentration so that
dramatists are effectively restricted to presenting a unified plot
which shows a conflict and its resolution.

The term 'epic', on the other hand, associated with the epics of
Homer (*The Odyssey*) and Virgil (*The Aeneid*), indicates work on a
grand scale, illustrating the story of a whole society. It has
normally been used about novels, indicating that the author is
recounting a story using as many episodes as is necessary to
contain his complete story. The term 'epic theatre' was first used in
Germany during the 1920s and is now firmly associated with
Brecht (and his friend and collaborator Erwin Piscator). Epic
theatre cuts across traditional divisions. Brecht found in epic
writing an objectivity, an ability of the author to stand back and
comment on the action, which attracted him. He wanted to make
his audience think, not just feel; to find ways of thinking that
would enable them to apply those processes to their real worlds
and therefore act as a force for change in society. And yet Brecht's
plays, whilst laying bare the wider concerns of mankind, are
constructed around characters whose stature is essentially small in
relation to their social and historical contexts.

In moving away from the conventional dramatic theatre, Brecht's
first change of emphasis was in the manner in which events were
presented to the audience. Instead of involving the audience,
persuading them to suspend their disbelief and become immersed in
the lives of the characters as they unfolded before them, Brecht
strove to ensure that his audience retained their critical judgement.
He wanted the audience to observe objectively what was
happening, aware of the alternatives that could have been followed.
Whereas the plot of a play for the dramatic theatre depended upon

closely intermeshed scenes that evolved apparently inexorably one from the other, the epic theatre presented scenes which moved in curves and jumps, making the audience think critically about what was unfolding before them.

In an essay written in 1936 but unpublished in his lifetime, Brecht distinguished between the spectator's attitude in the dramatic and epic theatres:

> The dramatic theatre's spectator says: Yes, I have felt like that too – Just like me – It's only natural – It'll never change – The sufferings of this man appal me, because they are inescapable – That's great art; it all seems the most obvious thing in the world – I weep when they weep, I laugh when they laugh.
>
> The epic theatre's spectator says: I'd never have thought it – That's not the way – That's extraordinary, hardly believable – It's got to stop – The sufferings of this man appal me, because they are unnecessary – That's great art; nothing obvious in it – I laugh when they weep, I weep when they laugh.
>
> (*Brecht on Theatre*, p. 71)

In order to achieve these objectives Brecht devised particular dramatic techniques which characterise his scripts and informed the productions of his plays, particularly as performed by the Berliner Ensemble.

Brecht was a very practical man who wrote plays with their production in mind. He was always prepared to modify or scrap ideas if they didn't work. Nevertheless understanding Brecht's theories is vital if a full understanding of his aims, intentions and achievements is to be arrived at. Avoiding the theory can lead to Brecht's innovations appearing to be just a series of technical gimmicks. In a statement made near the end of his life Brecht summed up his aims:

> My whole theory is much naiver than people think, or than my way of

putting it allows them to suppose. Perhaps I can excuse myself by
pointing to the case of Albert Einstein, who told the physicist Infield
that ever since boyhood he had merely reflected on the man running
after a ray of light and the man shut in a descending lift. And think
what complications that led to! I wanted to take the principle that it was
not just a matter of interpreting the world but of changing it, and apply
that to the theatre.

(*Brecht on Theatre*, p. 248)

Two points are worth noting here: firstly, that 'naive' is not a
pejorative term to Brecht; his aim was to make drama simpler, to
cut away confusions and complications. Secondly, Brecht's guiding
principle was drawn from Marx's *Theses on Feuerbach*: 'The
philosophers so far have only interpreted the world; the point,
however, is to change it.'

From this key principle emerge some of the most important of
Brecht's theatrical intentions:

- Since the world is all the time changing and capable of being
  changed, the playwright must neither assume nor allow his
  audience to assume that any phenomenon or activity is eternally
  obvious or uninteresting. The interest is in not just what happens
  but how and why. The playwright's job is to make the ordinary
  seem extraordinary by letting us see in a new way what we tend
  to dismiss as obvious.

- Brecht believed that audiences needed to be surprised because
  what they took for granted about life and the world was not
  necessarily unimportant or inevitable but was what they had
  been conditioned (usually unconsciously) to take for granted. The
  conditioning was done (again not necessarily consciously) by
  those who held power.

- His constant emphasis was that the audience should be actively
  critical rather than passively receptive of the play. He wanted to

use drama to help the audience to establish new ways of acting upon their 'real' world. He wanted to get rid of the ritual element in drama which involved submission to outside forces rather than an attempt to assess, criticise and control those forces.

- This meant that Brecht used his plays to weaken the hold of certain tendencies and ideas – such as fascism – and to strengthen others. In the struggle between classes, he was on the side of the underclass.

- The objectivity inherent in this approach meant that the audience could understand the actions and emotions of a given character and then be able to think about why such a character has behaved in such a way in that situation or why the situation has arisen. In opposing the established Aristotelian view of tragedy, in which the spectator participates in the drama and is purged of emotions by way of the pity and terror which the acting on stage evokes, Brecht challenged the view of the world in which men and women have little control over their destinies. Brecht's approach grew from and embodied his view of life as a struggle for emancipation, to enable the audience not to submit to power which is outside themselves and manipulates them for ends which are not theirs.

- Brecht also understood the need for drama to be entertaining – but he thought nothing was greater fun than finding out new things. He wanted to demystify the processes surrounding theatrical activity.

Brecht's intention was to develop a dialectical relationship with the audience, an interactive relationship involving the audience in consciously considering the situations and alternatives faced by the stage characters. Whereas the actor in naturalist theatre focused on the stage itself, the Brechtian actor's focus was the audience. His stage characters are not necessarily believable. In Brecht's plays it is not the actor's job to generate sympathy for, or antipathy towards, a character; their actions are to be examined critically from an emotional distance.

There are three key terms which Brecht coined to describe particular aspects of his epic or, as he later termed it, dialectical theatre:

1. Gest (or Gestus)

The development of the idea of *Gestus* became an essential link between Brecht's theory of acting and his practice as a playwright. It is a difficult word to interpret. The original, now obsolete, English word 'gest' meant 'bearing or carriage'. It would seem that Brecht wanted the one term to do a multiplicity of work. Brecht distinguished *Gestus* from gesture (*Geste*) by calling it

> a number of related gestures expressing such different attitudes as politeness, anger and so on.
>
> (*Brecht on Theatre*, p.246)

but also stated that:

> A language is gestic when it is grounded in a gest and conveys particular attitudes adopted by the speaker towards other men.
>
> (Ibid., p.104)

and of a song in the didactic play *The Mother*:

> The piece 'In Praise of Learning', which links the problem of learning with that of the working class's accession to power, is infected by the music with a heroic yet naturally cheerful gest.
>
> (Ibid., p.88)

and again:

> The realm of attitudes adopted by the characters towards one another is

what we call the realm of gest.

   (Ibid., p.198)

Trying to tie down a precise definition seems a thankless task and Brecht himself only occasionally saw an actor capable of gestic acting. He notes these occasions: Peter Lorre in *Man equals Man*, Charles Laughton in some parts of *Life of Galileo*, Helene Weigel in *The Mother* and *Mother Courage*. It is true to say that perfect 'gestic' acting would allow the meaning of a scene to be obvious even to an audience of the deaf.

Arnold Kettle's explanation of *Gestus*, in Unit 24 of the Open University course A3047 Drama, provides a clear insight into this quicksilver term:

> To Brecht a play is a series of *gests*. 'Each single incident has its basic *gest*.' Splitting the material he has to offer into one *gest* after another, the actor masters his character by first mastering the 'story'. Everything hangs on the 'story' which is in effect 'the complete fitting together of all the *gestic* incidents': but though each *gest* is in this basic sense only meaningful as part of the 'story', it is through the series of *gests* that the 'story' is revealed.

Brecht wrote:

> Gest is not supposed to mean gesticulation: it is not a matter of explanatory or emphatic movements of the hands, but of overall attitudes.
>
>   (*Brecht on Theatre*, p.104)

Kettle goes on to draw a link with the English word 'gist':

> The idea of *gest* also includes the notion that the text itself has to be seen as action and gesture, not as disembodied words. There is a sort of pun here with our own word 'gist'. The *gest*, you might say expresses the dialectical gist of the situation the dramatist is presenting.

2. *Verfremdung*

The translation of this term has also proved difficult. It has
sometimes been translated as 'alienation' but another German word
Entfremdung is normally used for this and it has a range of
meanings which do not match Brecht's intentions in using
Verfremdung. Basically the *Verfremdungseffekt* is Brecht's means
of controlling his audience's response so that they do not lose
themselves emotionally in the action but are forced into a
critical, thinking awareness. The effect is partly achieved by
the author's text itself, partly through the director's handling of
the text and partly through the actors' attitudes to what they
are doing.

The text itself:

- Setting the text in the past distances it.
- Avoiding rhetorical language except in very special circumstances.
- Constructing the whole play in the form of a story (epic) as
  opposed to giving it the structure of an individual's emotional
  crisis.

The director's approach:

- The stage is treated strictly as a stage. The curtain should not
  conceal everything (e.g. scene shifting) but should allow the
  audience to be aware that work is going on. Lights are not
  concealed. The illusion that is created must always be recognised
  as an illusion so that reality is turned into art and can be seen to
  be alterable.
- A summary of the action of the scene about to be presented may
  be projected on a screen before the scene.
- Filmstrips, videos, projections may be used for purposes of
  background, information and to link stage events with reality.
- The setting in terms of the whole stage picture is important

because it creates an illusion and yet limits its essential elements.
- Open use of technology and stage mechanics (e.g. revolving stage) can assist the *V-effekt*.
- All of the details presented on stage should be realistic – much more trouble should be taken to get these absolutely right than may be the case for naturalistic plays. This is shown clearly in the opening lines of Brecht's poem 'Weigel's props':

> Just as the millet farmer picks out for his trial plot
> The heaviest seeds and the poet
> The exact words for his verse so
> She selects the objects to accompany
> Her characters across the stage.
>
> (Trans. John Willett, *Poems 1913–1956*, p.427)

The songs: Although integrated into the text, songs are performed within a convention different from that of the rest of the play (see Brecht's Notes, pp. 86–7 of this edition). The singers, Brecht explained, were openly 'the playwright's own accomplices', using the 'sister art' to make points which could not be made in the same way within the normal text. Brecht had this to say about the use of music in an epic theatre production, with particular reference to *The Threepenny Opera*:

> The musical items, which had the immediacy of a ballad, were of a reflective and moralizing nature. The play showed the close relationship between the emotional life of the bourgeois and that of the criminal world. The criminals showed, sometimes through the music itself, that their sensations, feelings and prejudices were the same as those of the average citizen and theatregoer. One theme was, broadly speaking, to show that the only pleasant life is a comfortably-off one, even if this involves doing without certain 'higher things'. A love duet was used to argue that superficial circumstances like the social origin of one's partner

or her economic status should have no influence on a man's matrimonial decisions. A trio expressed concern at the fact that the uncertainties of life on this planet apparently prevent the human race from following its natural inclinations towards goodness and decent behaviour. The tenderest and most moving love-song in the play described the eternal, indestructible mutual attachment of a procurer and his girl. The lovers sang, not without nostalgia, of their little home, the brothel. In such ways, the music, just because it took up a purely emotional attitude and spurned none of the stock narcotic attractions, became an active collaborator in the stripping bare of the middle class corpus of ideas. It became, so to speak, a muck-raker, an informer, a nark.

(*Brecht on Theatre*, pp.85–6)

The actors: The Brechtian actor is trained not to 'immerse himself' in his part but to understand it and its role in the social situation depicted by the play. This does not mean that the actor does not think himself into his part but it does mean that he is discouraged from becoming possessed by it. The task of a Brechtian actor is to understand and communicate, not to empathise and be transformed. This point is made clearly in Brecht's poem, 'The moment before impact':

I speak my lines before
The audience hears them; what they will hear is
Something done with. Every word that leaves the lip
Describes an arc, and then
Falls on the listener's ear; I wait and hear
The way it strikes; I know
We are not feeling the same thing and
We are not feeling it at the same time.

(Trans. Edith Anderson, *Poems 1913–1956*, p.342)

Clear contrasts are evident with the naturalistic Stanislavskian approach. These differences can be seen in Brecht's response to what he cited as a typically 'naturalistic' description by the actor Rapaport:

> On the stage the actor is surrounded entirely by fictions ... The actor must be able to regard all this as though it were true, as though he were convinced that all that surrounds him on stage is a living reality and, along with himself, he must convince the audience as well. This is the central feature of our method of work on the part ... Take any object, a cap for example; lay it on the table or on the floor and try to regard it as though it were a rat: make believe that it is a rat, not a cap ... Picture what sort of rat it is; what size, colour? ... We thus commit ourselves to believe quite naively that the object before us is something other than it is and, at the same time, learn to compel the audience to believe.
>
> (*Brecht on Theatre*, p.142)

Brecht rejected this approach outright:

> This might be thought to be a course of instruction for conjurers but in fact it is a course of acting, supposedly according to Stanislavsky's method. One wonders if a technique that equips an actor to make an audience see rats where there aren't any can really be all that suitable for disseminating the truth. Given enough alcohol it doesn't take acting to persuade almost anybody that he is seeing rats: pink ones.

In battling against the 'culinary' theatre, Brecht sought to establish a realist approach. In an essay 'The Popular and the Realistic', he set out a list of criteria for his definition of realism:

Brecht's criteria	Interpretation
Laying bare society's causal network	Showing the audience the ways in which human action is determined by people's social positions and expectations
Showing up the dominant viewpoint as the viewpoint of the dominators	Revealing that what are assumed to be eternal truths are simply views that reinforce the power of those in power
Writing from the standpoint of the class which has prepared the broadest solutions for the most pressing problems afflicting human society	Championing the working class by showing their capacity to resolve basic issues of survival
Emphasising the dynamics of development	Revealing the nature of the relationship between one action and another
Concrete and so as to encourage abstraction	Creating specific characters and stories played in such a way as to make the audience think

(*Brecht on Theatre*, p.109)

Brecht was intensely aware of the ways in which what is familiar protects itself from criticism by its unobtrusiveness. The *Verfremdungseffekte* were designed to expose the familiar – Brecht's actors were to present things in their concrete reality so that the audience would be encouraged to think about what had given rise to the situation depicted and therefore consider ways to change those conditions in future. (See also Brecht's notes 'Hints for actors', p. 84–6.)

3. Montage

Brecht's concept of 'epic' involved the principle of montage, of creating a play which showed one thing after another and where each scene existed for itself; where the links between events were deliberately severed, generating a series of isolated images which the audience had to work to connect. A performance would be broken down into clearly marked segments.

Montage theory had been developed by Russian and American film makers, perhaps most explicitly by the Soviet film director, Sergei Eisenstein. The term first appeared in his 1923 essay 'Montazh attraktsionov' (Montage of Attractions). It referred to the circus-style series of episodic 'turns' which characterised his re-worked version of Ostrovsky's nineteenth-century classic *Enough Stupidity in Every Wise Man*, staged as a satirico-political clown show, with acrobatics, high-wire stunts and filmed inserts. He later adapted his ideas to the editing of film – the intercutting and juxtaposition of unrelated but emotive images which produce a heightened political perception in the observer. Probably the most famous example is the 'Odessa Steps' sequence in *Battleship Potemkin* where Eisenstein intercut the image of stamping military boots with pictures of a pram, containing a baby, careering down the steps. In the original manifesto, an 'attraction' was defined as

> any aggressive moment in theatre, i.e. any element of it that subjects the audience to emotional or psychological influence, verified by experience and mathematically calculated to produce specific emotional shocks in the spectator in their proper order within the whole. These shocks provide the only opportunity of perceiving the ideological aspect of what is being shown, the final ideological conclusion.

Eisenstein pointed out that if one fragment of a woman dressed in black is shown and that fragment is followed by another, a photo of a grave, the viewer of these two discreet fragments would then mentally telescope them into an image of a widow. In other words, the spectator provides continuity. Earlier, the American director, D.W. Griffith, had introduced a technique of film cutting that jumped from scene to scene deliberately leaving out segments of the action and relying on the spectator to make an unbroken transition from scene A to B to C and so on. Brecht insisted that Peter Lorre in the 1931 production of *Man equals Man* adopt a style of acting that created this montage technique. When Lorre's performance was criticised for being exaggerated, disjointed and impersonal – for example when Lorre was supposed to express chalk-white fear at the prospect of his imminent execution, he turned his back on the audience, dipped his hands in a bowl of white chalk, smeared it on his face, and abruptly turned again to confront the audience – Brecht leapt to his defence, arguing that the unity of type or character in the role came about 'despite, or rather by means of interruptions and jumps'. Responding to the challenge that Peter Lorre was 'short-winded and episodic', Brecht replied that the actor 'links all these single episodes together and absorbs them in the combined flow of his role'. Lorre was attempting to match the stress on breaks with stress on continuity. It is important to remember that Brecht's plays are crafted in such a way as to ensure that the breaks are always offset by carefully structured elements to establish their continuity and build bridges across the gaps.

Thus montage can be seen as a crucial element in challenging the audience to think, to make connections and to realise the need for action beyond the theatre.

> The stage began to be instructive.
>
> Oil, inflation, war, social struggles, the family, religion, wheat, the meat market, all became subjects for theatrical representation. Choruses enlightened the spectator. ... Films showed a montage of events from all over the world. Projections added statistical material. And as the 'background' came to the front of the stage so people's activity was subjected to criticism ... The theatre became an affair for philosophers,

but only such philosophers as wished not just to explain the world but also to change it.

   (*Brecht on Theatre*, pp.71–2)

In so far as this affects a production of *The Threepenny Opera*, the montage element is helped by the use of titles and screens:

> The screens on which the titles of each scene are projected are a primitive attempt at literarizing the theatre [. . .] Some exercise in complex seeing is needed – though it is perhaps more important to be able to think above the stream than to think in [i.e. within] the stream. Moreover the use of screens imposes and facilitates a new style of acting. This style is the epic style. As he reads the projections on the screen the spectator adopts an attitude of smoking-and-watching. [. . .] By these means one would soon have a theatre full of experts, just as one has a sporting arena full of experts. No chance of the actors having the effrontery to offer such people those few miserable scraps of imitation which they at present cook up in a few rehearsals 'any old how' and without the least thought!
>
>   (*Brecht on Theatre*, pp.43–4)

Historical background to *The Threepenny Opera*

In 1918 Britain emerged from the First World War victorious and with its economy and Empire relatively intact, but Germany was in turmoil. The Treaty of Versailles, signed on 28 June 1919, imposed humiliating terms on the defeated German nation. The Kaiser, Wilhelm II, had abdicated two days before the armistice signed on 11 November 1918 brought an immediate end to hostilities. He went into exile the following year. The armistice had been signed on Germany's behalf by a Socialist Council of People's Representatives, and a Soviet-style revolution in Germany seemed a distinct possibility. These revolutionary possibilities centred on a group called the Spartacists led by two radical socialists – Rosa

Luxemburg and Karl Liebknecht. However, in February 1919, a
National Constituent Assembly gathered in the town of Weimar,
where a republican constitution for the country was worked out
which provided for a seven-year presidential term, two chambers of
government, proportional representation and a guarantee of federal
rights which paved the way for what became the Weimar Republic,
which lasted from 1919 until 1933.

The new government, under President Ebert, took on the
obligations of the Versailles Treaty, which included territorial
concessions, loss of colonies, limitations on the army and
armaments, as well as crippling payments to the victorious powers
(known as reparations). The immediate result was economic crisis
and revolt. The army was used to suppress the Spartacists before
they could consolidate their power. During street fighting in Berlin,
both Luxemburg and Liebknecht were killed and although members
of the group had founded the German Communist Party in
December 1918 the heart was torn out of the revolutionary
movement. Meanwhile, despite the names of groups like the
'German Workers' Party', which implied that the working classes
would be in control, these were actually right-wing forces which
began to unite around an appeal to German nationalist sentiment.
Adolf Hitler joined the GWP in 1919 and renamed it National
Socialist German Workers' Party. By the mid-twenties, almost 45
million Germans were living on incomes normally paid to
labourers, when the actual size of the working class (judged on the
basis of type of work and other social criteria) was only 25
million.

The economic situation in the early 1920s was spiralling out of
control and giving rise to galloping inflation. In 1914 one dollar
had been worth about four Reichsmarks; by 1922 this had become
7,000, and, by 1923, several million. The middle classes, who
tended to be those who lost all their savings and assets during this
inflationary period, were politicised by these events and were

thrown into the arms of any party which sought to represent their sense of disaffection. Having become leader of the NSGWP (which later became the National Socialist (Nazi) Party), Hitler attempted to seize political power by staging a so-called 'putsch' in Munich, in November 1923. It failed and Hitler was given a brief prison sentence.

Between 1923 and 1929, Germany enjoyed a period of relative calm and even a degree of prosperity, brought about by the stabilisation of the currency through the introduction of the Rentenmark, the spreading out of reparations, and massive injections of American capital. By 1927 unemployment, for example, had sunk as low as 300,000. However the recovery was short-lived and the depression years of 1929-31 in the wake of the collapse of the stock market in America (the so-called Wall Street Crash) led to a worsening economic crisis and mass unemployment. The way was open for Hitler to make his second, more subtle, attempt to seize power. He had set out his ideas in the first volume of his political autobiography *Mein Kampf* (My Struggle), published in 1925, which first broached the basic ingredients of Nazi ideology – a mixture of anti-semitism, exaggeration of the communist menace, the need for centralised government, denunciation of the Treaty of Versailles and the promise of a vigorously nationalistic foreign policy. The second volume came out in 1927. By January 1933 it had sold 287,000 copies. After 1933, when Hitler had become Chancellor of Germany, it is estimated that around 10,000,000 copies of *Mein Kampf* were in circulation. Relevant to this is the fact that, between September 1929 and September 1932, the number of registered unemployed rose from 1.3 million to 5.1 million. As if in response to this, between the 1928 and July 1932 elections, the Nazi vote increased from 800,000 to 13,750,000, i.e. from 2.16 per cent of the national poll to 37.3. These final years of the decade were critical ones, beginning with the production of *The Threepenny Opera* in Berlin, and ending with Hitler's elevation to the Chancellorship and his inauguration of the Third Reich. Berlin was the city at the centre of these events.

Life in Berlin

In the 1920s, the city of Berlin was not just the centre of Germany but the cultural metropolis of Europe, whose brashly decadent and dangerously politicised mood was recreated in the 1972 film *Cabaret*, based on Christopher Isherwood's novel *Goodbye to Berlin* (1939). The English poet W.H. Auden and his friend, Christopher Isherwood, were attracted to Berlin in the 1920s precisely because it was the antithesis of London. The Weimar Republic had experienced a revolution in manners and morals brought about by the war which had produced profound changes in social behaviour, religion, sexual mores and commercial practice, and where the spirit of freedom and experimentation both in personal affairs and in the arts was epitomised by extreme forms of modernist painting and drama exemplified by the Expressionist movement.

However, this was counterbalanced by a contrasting spirit of sobriety, practicality, and scientific method which characterised an emerging modern world of assembly lines, time-and-motion studies, automobiles, aeroplanes, mass observation and psychoanalysis – everything, in fact, captured by another term which belonged to 1920s Germany, 'Die Neue Sachlichkeit', or 'The New Objectivity'. This approach rejected the emotional extremes of Expressionism in favour of a more restrained, scientifically detached attitude to the world. However, the general mood of Germany's capital remained feverish and chaotic, so much so that when Hitler's eventual Minister for Propaganda, Joseph Goebbels, arrived in Berlin in 1926 to take charge of the local Nazi organisation, he observed: 'This city is a melting-pot of everything that is evil – prostitution, drinking houses, cinemas, Marxism, Jews, strippers, negroes dancing and all the off-shoots of modern art.' He might also have mentioned that the city was a magnet for homosexuals who, together with Jews and gypsies, became prominent targets for the Nazis.

A year later, Berlin boasted 49 theatres, over 70 cabarets and nightclubs as well as three opera houses. By 1929 it had over 300 cinemas and more than 2,630 newspapers, magazines and journals of various kinds. The black American entertainer Josephine Baker danced naked for private audiences or appeared before packed houses dressed only in a skirt made of bananas. Avant-garde artists who gathered at their favourite cafés included the likes of George Grosz and Otto Dix whose grotesquely distorted images of Berlin low life and bourgeois high life found theatrical expression in a work like *The Threepenny Opera*.

Theatrical background to *The Threepenny Opera*

The composition and production of *The Threepenny Opera* came about as a result of a number of factors, chief among which were Brecht's association with the theatre director Erich Engel, his membership of a theatre collective established by the communist theatre director Erwin Piscator, his meeting Kurt Weill for the first time, and a fortuitous encounter with a young actor, Ernst-Josef Aufricht, who was trying to open his own theatre. Engel had already directed Brecht's version of Marlowe's *Edward II* in 1925 and was to direct *Man equals Man* in 1928. There had been a radio broadcast of the latter work in 1927 about which Weill wrote an enthusiastic review. The composer had also been impressed by a volume of ironic verse *Die Hauspostille* (*Devotions*) which Brecht had recently published. Having met each other in the spring of 1927, Brecht and Weill decided to collaborate on a 'Mahagonny Opera', with its notion of a 'paradise city', utilising some of the

'Mahagonny Songs' in the *Devotions*. What became known as *The Little Mahagonny* (as distinct from the later collaborative work *The Rise and Fall of the City of Mahagonny*) was performed in the summer of 1927 during a German chamber music festival in Baden-Baden. Brecht and Weill then agreed on further collaborations at the same time as the former was working with others on an adaptation of Jaroslav Hašek's satirical First World War novel *The Good Soldier Schweik* for Piscator and his designer George Grosz. However, further plans to work with Piscator seemed unlikely to be realised because of the director's overstretched finances, so Brecht started to look elsewhere. This is where Aufricht came into the picture.

At the beginning of 1928, Ernst-Josef Aufricht had been given a present of 100,000 marks by his father with which to set up his own theatre. He began by renting the Theater am Schiffbauerdamm and hired Erich Engel to direct a play to celebrate his own twenty-eighth birthday. However he had not been able to find anyone to write a new play for him until he was introduced, by chance, to Brecht in a Berlin café. When asked whether he had any work in progress, Brecht seized the opportunity and proposed a play based on John Gay's *The Beggar's Opera*, which Elisabeth Hauptmann had translated, suggesting that Kurt Weill could compose new music to replace the eighteenth-century ballads. In fact work on 'Scum', as it was originally entitled before it became 'The Pimp's Opera' and then *The Threepenny Opera*, was at little more than the planning stage. Aufricht liked the idea but was worried that Weill's music might prove too modernistic; he therefore made contingency plans to recycle Pepusch's original score for *The Beggar's Opera* if necessary. His worries proved unfounded, although circumstances surrounding preparations for the play's premiere were not propitious.

There were so many problems leading up to the first night that it seemed highly unlikely that *The Threepenny Opera* would prove a great theatrical success. First of all the play and the music had to be written. Rehearsals were then rushed; the distance between the first one and the premiere on 31 August 1928 being less than a month. Orchestral rehearsals did not begin until 25th. Throughout, Brecht and Weill continued to revise or add to the playscript and musical score. Matters were not helped by a number of minor and major crises. Carola Neher, who was due to play Polly, had to go to Switzerland to tend to her dying husband, the poet Klabund, with the result that she arrived two weeks late for rehearsal and felt obliged to abandon the role. She was replaced by Roma Bahn who learned the part in four days. Then a new Mr Peachum had to be recruited in the shape of Erich Ponto. Mrs Peachum (Rosa Valetti) objected to having to sing 'The Ballad of Sexual Obsession' so the song was cut. Helene Weigel developed appendicitis and so her role as Mrs Coaxer, the brothel madame, was cut from the play and never replaced. The actress playing Lucy found some of the music in Scene Eight, which Weill had composed with another singer in mind, too difficult, with the result that this was also cut, as was the scene itself at a later date. The 'Solomon Song' was dropped because the play's running-time was too long and, at the last minute, Lotte Lenya's name was accidentally left off the cast list – an omission which infuriated her husband Kurt Weill – and a programme insert had to be provided identifying her in the role of Jenny.

Macheath (Harald Paulsen) proved difficult to direct. A matinee idol who had made his name in cabaret and had a fervent female following, he insisted on wearing a blue bow tie. Instead of making an issue of this, however, Brecht turned Paulsen's vanity to shrewd advantage: 'Let's leave him as he is, oversweet and charming. Weill and I will introduce him with a *Moritat* that tells of his gruesome and disgraceful deeds. The effect made by the light-blue bow will be all the more curious' (Jürgen Schebera, *Kurt Weill: An Illustrated Life*, New Haven and London, Yale University Press,

1995, pp.107-8). Thus, the play's greatest musical hit came about almost by accident and was also composed at the last minute. On the actual opening night, nervous tension was high and the expectation of failure seemed to be confirmed by the first night audience's silent response to the early scenes. However, following the 'Cannon Song', the audience suddenly burst into enthusiastic applause and the cast gradually began to realise they had a hit on their hands.

According to Jürgen Rühle,

> [*The Threepenny Opera*'s] insolence and tough cynicism reflected an era poised on the brink of an abyss. The smiling irony of the country fair and the bordello romanticism of Soho, with its colorful collection of crooks, gangsters, whores and beggars, its travesty of kitsch, its impudent, ear-splitting songs [coupled with] Kurt Weill's exciting music – a mixture of hurdy-gurdy sentimentality and brassy jazz – and finally, its timely, detached social criticism, all these served to captivate an audience.
>
> (Jürgen Rühle, *Literature and Revolution*, London, Pall Mall Press, 1969, p.222)

The production was given a hostile reception by the *Völkische Beobachter*, Hitler's news-sheet, which considered that its crudity appeared redolent of 'the moral cesspool, found in some form in every large city, [which] may be just the thing for the movie romanticism of the underworld but otherwise is of interest only to the sanitation department' (ibid.). Another conservative paper 'claimed to hear in the noisy, pounding rhythm of the music "the approach of the class-conscious Bolshevik battalions"'.

The way had been prepared for a work such as *The Threepenny Opera* by a vogue for the experimental in the arts. Arthur Schnitzler's play *Der Reigen* (*The Round Dance*, better known by its film title *La Ronde*) had been taken to court on charges of immorality as early as 1920, as had Walter Hasenclever's play

Marriages are Made in Heaven (1928) – the latter for 'undermining Christian values'. With the First World War fresh in mind, George Grosz was charged with blasphemy for depicting Jesus wearing a gas mask. Erwin Piscator outraged critics for similarly unpatriotic reasons by staging *The Adventures of the Good Soldier Schweik* (1928), which not only satirised German militarism but also brought a latrine on stage which, pursuing Goebbels' obsessional imagery, was characterised by a reviewer as 'disquisitions from the cesspool'. Riots attended performances of Ernst Toller's *Hinkemann*, which showed a war veteran in a fairground cage eating rats for the entertainment of paying customers. At the same time, the experimental theatre received technical inspiration from a new school of art, architecture and design founded in Weimar by Walter Gropius and called the Bauhaus. Its first exhibition, in 1923, included a programme of musical works by Stravinsky and Hindemith and a concert of Dadaist music with improvised jazz, all of which influenced Kurt Weill and made an impact on his music for *The Threepenny Opera*. The German branch of the Dadaists, a group dedicated to making provocative, nihilistic artistic statements, could usually be found at one of their regular Berlin haunts – the Romanisches Café on Tauenzienstrasse.

Also relevant to the anti-bourgeois spirit of *The Threepenny Opera* are the sentiments of someone like Kurt Tucholsky, who declared:

> Since 1913 I have belonged to those people who believe that the German spirit is poisoned almost beyond recovery, who do not believe in an improvement, who regard German democracy as a façade and a lie, and who, despite all assurances and optimistic touches, believe that an empty steel helmet is not as dangerous as a silk hat.
> (Cited in Gordon A. Craig, *Germany 1866-1945*, Oxford University Press, 1981, pp. 485–6)

The question could be asked whether *The Threepenny Opera* was actually too enjoyable to be a serious attack on bourgeois morality and capitalist property rights but in its revolutionary mixing of highbrow and lowbrow elements to form a new kind of musical theatre it made a radical assault on accepted norms.

The Beggar's Opera

Brecht's *Threepenny Opera* might never have existed without the successful revival of John Gay's *The Beggar's Opera* in 1920. Staged by Nigel Playfair at the Lyric Theatre, Hammersmith, and designed by Lovat Fraser, this revival ran non-stop for 1,463 performances over three-and-a-half years. It was news of this production which caused Elisabeth Hauptmann, Brecht's collaborator, to prepare a translation of Gay's opera in 1927, which became the basis for Brecht's version, *The Threepenny Opera*. This premiered in August 1928 and brought him his greatest box office success.

The Beggar's Opera presents, in a colourful description of eighteenth-century London low life, the story of Captain Macheath, leader of a gang of highwaymen, who is also a womaniser. He secretly marries Polly Peachum, the daughter of a receiver of stolen goods. His disapproving in-laws plot to have him arrested, believing that he will be hanged and that they will be able to get their hands on his ill-gotten gains which their daughter will inherit. However, unknown to them (and to Polly) Macheath is also engaged to Lucy Lockit, daughter of the gaoler of Newgate prison where Macheath is held following his arrest. To Macheath's dismay, Polly and Lucy meet, but despite being horrified by his deceitful behaviour, Lucy helps him to escape. He is recaptured, but the Beggar arrives in time to engineer an unexpected happy ending.

The Beggar's Opera was premiered on 29 January 1728 and ran for 90 consecutive performances, an almost unprecedented success at a time when productions tended to have short runs, irrespective of their success, because of contemporary audiences' desire for novelty. The main character, Macheath, was modelled after two famous London criminals, Jack Sheppard and Jonathan Wild, while Peachum was given traits of the then prime minister, Robert Walpole. According to Gay, the message was 'High life equals low life' and that throughout 'the whole piece you may observe such a similitude of manners in high and low life, that it is difficult to determine whether (in the fashionable vices) the fine Gentleman imitates the Gentleman of the Road [i.e. the highwayman] or the Gentleman of the Road the fine Gentleman' (cited in Karl H. Schoeps, *Bertolt Brecht*, New York, Frederick Ungar, 1977, p.121).

The Beggar's Opera takes place at the beginning of the eighteenth century, a period which saw the rise of the bourgeoisie. As William Empson wrote in 1935, 'The main joke is not against the characters of the play at all [...] it is against the important people who are *like* the characters; the main thing is the political attack and the principles behind it' (*Some Versions of Pastoral*, Harmondsworth, Penguin Books, 1966, p. 159). He also suggests that, 'The thieves and whores parody the aristocratic ideal, [while Peachum, Lockit and their families] parody the bourgeois ideal [...] these two ideals are naturally at war, and the rise to power of the bourgeois had made the war important' (ibid., p.175).

The Beggar's Opera was not a serious opera in the accepted tradition of the time. In 1724, the German composer George Frideric Handel, who had settled in England, composed an opera *Giulio Cesare* (Julius Caesar) and in the following year *Rodelinda*. Both these operas were examples of the 'opera seria', literally 'serious opera', which dealt with dignified subjects, often of a mythological nature and featuring elaborate arias and complicated choral singing. The story was told in 'recitative' (i.e. stylised, semi-spoken dialogue usually to harpsichord accompaniment) and tended to be in Italian. However, at the same time as Handel was working

on these more formal operas, a Scot called Allan Ramsay was
writing a more lighthearted 'ballad opera', *The Gentle Shepherd,*
which was in English and consisted of everyday spoken dialogue
interspersed with popular songs supplied with new words to fit the
plot. Ramsay was not the first in the field, however, as one
Thomas Durfey had composed a similar work using folk melodies
as early as 1706. Ramsay's work was not actually performed until
1730, two years after the premiere of *The Beggar's Opera.*

The background to the composition of *The Beggar's Opera*
consisted of these influences but also owed a debt to the famous
satirist and author of *Gulliver's Travels*, Jonathan Swift, who wrote
to the poet, Alexander Pope, asking him what he thought of the
idea of a 'Newgate pastoral' set among whores and thieves. By
'Newgate' he meant the famous prison on the site of what is now
the Central Criminal Court, the Old Bailey; by 'pastoral' he meant
a highly conventional mode of writing which celebrated the
innocent life of shepherds and shepherdesses in an idealised Golden
Age, which went back to the Greeks of the third century BC. The
tradition was revived in the sixteenth century – in England by
Philip Sidney, Edmund Spenser, Christopher Marlowe and others.
It is obviously ironic to refer to a 'pastoral' about less than
innocent thieves and whores in a prison setting.

The idea appealed to John Gay who wrote the text and selected
the ballads, which he borrowed from Thomas Durfey and a
sourcebook of folk music from Scotland, Ireland and France. He
also borrowed from 'professional' composers such as Henry Purcell
and Jeremiah Clarke as well as Handel. Purcell's patriotic song
'Britons, Strike Home', for example, became Macheath's 'Since I
must swing I scorn to wince and whine', and the highwaymen's
anthem to their trade of robbery, 'Let us take the road', is a
pastiche of a march tune from Handel's *Rodelinda*. Gay's original
idea was that the songs should be unaccompanied, but the manager
of the Theatre at Lincoln's Inn Fields where the play was

performed insisted there be an orchestra. The result was that an émigré German, Johann Christoph Pepusch, was persuaded to score the music of the opera for a small orchestra as well as write an overture.

Swift was pleased with the result:

> This comedy contains ... a satire [...] where the author takes the occasion of comparing the common robbers of the public and their several stratagems for betraying, undermining and hanging each other, to the several arts of the politicians in times of corruption. This comedy likewise exposes, with great justice, that taste for Italian music among us, which is wholly unsuitable to the northern climate and the genius of the people.
>
> (Quoted in Phoebe Fenwick Gaye, *John Gay – His Place in the Eighteenth Century,* London, Collins, 1938, p.341)

An aspect of pastoral satire in *The Beggar's Opera* can be seen in the presence of a good deal of bird and animal imagery which is conspicuously absent from Brecht's play. However, there are also blasphemous elements – such as the parallels between Macheath's fate and Christ's – which Brecht elaborates in the more obviously religious satirical context of *The Threepenny Opera*. In Gay's opera there is a subtly worked metaphorical strand which connects sex with death and judicial hanging, with the punning implication that women like to see their men 'well hung'. Brecht picks up on this but does not emphasise it to the extent that Gay does. As Empson suggests in connection with the Gay work:

> as most literature uses the idea of our eventual death as a sort of frame or test for its conception of happiness, so this play uses hanging. [...] Hanging in the songs may even become a sort of covert metaphor for true love [he quotes a line from a song by Polly which concludes 'The true love's knot they faster bind']. It is the hangman's knot, and the irony goes on echoing through the play [...] it uses the connexion between death (here hanging) and the sexual act, which is not merely a

favourite of Freud but a common joke of the period.

(Op. cit., pp.179–81)

Or as Lucy sings to Macheath in Act Two, scene 18,

When you come to the tree, should the hangman refuse,
These fingers, with pleasure, could fasten the noose,

a sentiment which also includes a reference to Christ, where the
cross and 'the tree' are synonymous, as well as connecting with the
gallows.

Stephen Hinton summarises the important distinctions which
need to be made between the two works:

Unlike in *The Beggar's Opera*, the outrage expressed in *The Threepenny
Opera* is general, not particular. Werner Hecht has reduced the
differences between the two works to a pair of neat and beguiling
formulations: '1728: veiled critique of an open state of affairs, 1928: open
critique of a veiled state of affairs'. Gay's satire contains scarcely
camouflaged barbs against the Walpole administration, whereas Weill and
Brecht's satire lampoons conventional bourgeois morality, both in and
out of the theatre.

(Hinton, p.189)

Moreover, in Gay's work the capture of Macheath is a high
dramatic point of the opera. Brecht deliberately seeks to avoid this
kind of dramatic structure, which builds to a contrived climax, by
having Macheath arrested twice.

Among other changes, Brecht substitutes High Sheriff Brown for
Lockit and re-names his daughter Lucy Brown. He cuts the
Beggar's Introduction and assigns his role as *deus ex machina* at
the end to Brown. He cuts the number of songs drastically, as well
as cutting the tavern scenes, the dance to harp accompaniment in
Act Two, a dance of prisoners in chains and a general dance at the
end. He also cuts scenes in a gaming house and in Peachum's
'lock', or banking house. He sets the marriage of Macheath and
Polly in a stable, renders Mrs Peachum sober rather than

permanently drunk, makes Lucy's pregnancy false rather than real
and stages Macheath's first arrest in a brothel.

Lastly, it might be mentioned that Gay's *The Beggar's Opera* has
continued to influence other dramatists and artists generally,
especially since Brecht's adaptation breathed fresh contemporary
life into it. These include the German film maker Rainer
Fassbinder, the Czech dramatist (and subsequent president of the
Czech Republic) Vaclav Havel, the Czech film maker Jiri Wenzel,
the British Alan Ayckbourn (*A Chorus of Disapproval*, 1984) and
the Nigerian Wole Soyinka's *Opera Wonyosi* (1977).

Kurt Weill, music and song

Brecht was always happy to borrow and re-work the material of
other writers and dramatists – an eclectic magpie, it could be said.
He was also an extremely willing and perceptively selective
collaborator, especially in the field of music. Probably his most
well-known 'partner' was the composer Kurt Weill who
collaborated with him on *The Little Mahagonny, The Threepenny
Opera, Happy End, The Rise and Fall of the City of Mahagonny,
The Seven Deadly Sins,* and *He Said Yes/He Said No.* Weill was
born in the German town of Dessau in 1900 and first studied
music in his native city before making his first attempt at operatic
writing at the age of sixteen. After studying philosophy at Berlin
University he took lessons in musical composition with the
German composer Humperdinck (of *Hansel and Gretel* fame). He
had the opportunity to conduct opera but could not go to Vienna
to study under the most renowned musical modernist, Arnold
Schoenberg, because he didn't have the necessary money. Instead
he studied with the relatively obscure and highly individual Italian
composer Ferruccio Busoni, whose classes he attended in Berlin for
three years. Busoni was particularly interested in re-evaluating the
genius of Mozart and especially his *The Magic Flute.* The score of

The Threepenny Opera does in fact contain a number of quotations and echoes of that Mozart opera. In the finale to Act One, Peachum sings a phrase of the birdcatcher Papageno from the Act One quintet, and in the finale, the Messenger recalls the wise Sarastro, while Macheath even borrows some phrases from the soprano role of the heroine, Pamina. Busoni also encouraged his students to reject the influence of Wagner whose work was very popular at the time. Weill's reaction against Wagner is apparent in the 'Pirate Jenny' song which is a kind of parody of Senta's ballad in Wagner's *The Flying Dutchman*.

Weill completed his first opera, *The Protagonist,* in 1925, on which he collaborated with the dramatist Georg Kaiser. This was followed by *Royal Palace,* in collaboration with the surrealist poet, Iwan Goll, which was the first of his stage works to include popular dance music (the foxtrot and ragtime) and the non-orchestral instrument, the saxophone, which was especially associated with jazz. His next opera, *The Tsar Has His Photograph Taken* (1927) was another collaboration with Kaiser, but it was the 'Songspiel' (Songplay) *Mahagonny* composed the same year that saw his first collaboration with Brecht and marked the emergence of a distinctive 'song-style'. What brought the two men together was less their political sympathies (Weill did not have Brecht's interest in Marxist theory) than their interest in writing a full-scale opera with a difference. After further collaborations however, their partnership broke up in 1931, never to be resumed. As a Jew, Weill felt directly threatened by Hitler's rise to power so he decided to leave the country, together with his wife Lotte Lenya, first settling in Paris, then in 1935, in New York, where he decided to become a Broadway composer. His *Knickerbocker Holiday* (1938) is remembered for the beautifully haunting ballad 'September Song'. *We Will Never Die,* staged in 1943, was dedicated 'to the two million Jewish dead of Europe', which by the end of the war had risen to six million. His *Lost in the Stars*

(1949) was based on the South African novelist, Alan Paton's *Cry the Beloved Country*. It was clear that Weill had managed to add an extra dimension of sophistication to the American musical genre as well as drawing on American folk and dance music. His opera based on Elmer Rice's play *Street Scene* (1947) seemed to many to embody the best of his aspirations for a popular yet authentic form of musical theatre. He died of a heart attack in 1950 while working with the dramatist Maxwell Anderson on a musical version of Mark Twain's *Huckleberry Finn*.

Weill and Brecht's model for *The Threepenny Opera*, John Gay's *The Beggar's Opera*, had deliberately turned its back on the taste for classical opera in the style of Handel in favour of something more popular and down-to-earth. In just the same way, Kurt Weill set himself the task of replacing the large-scale operas like those of Wagner and Richard Strauss, which centred on myths and were regarded as 'high art', with something altogether more accessible and singable. This was to be an opera for amateurs rather than professionals, which did not require either a trained operatic soprano voice or the vocal pyrotechnics of a 'Heldentenor' (heroic tenor) in the leading roles. However, although the music was meant to be accessible to amateurs, this did not mean that it was any less subtle or less complex than that of Weill's classical contemporaries, such as Arnold Schoenberg and Alban Berg. It was just different and open to other kinds of influence, both ancient and modern.

Although Mozart wrote operas on classical themes for court and upper-class audiences, some of which were also based on remote myth and legend, Weill felt the need to return to the essentially popular spirit of works such as *The Magic Flute*, with its pantomimic overtones, and *The Marriage of Figaro*. In *The Magic Flute* Mozart's reliance on simple song-forms resulted in the direct communication of simple and important human feelings and experiences. The form of Mozartian opera, which was considered

old-fashioned by the Modernists, appealed to Weill in so far as the
music and the words (in the form of recitative) remained separate.
For Weill, Mozart was the operatic composer *par excellence*, and
he believed that the future of opera lay in the revival of the
eighteenth-century opera of musical 'numbers' interspersed with
spoken dialogue. In Weill's opinion, Wagner's art expressed only
the feelings of larger-than-life figures. A return to the *Singspiel*
would also be a return to real life. This was the pattern which
Weill and Brecht adopted for *The Threepenny Opera*. It gave them
the opportunity, not only to emphasise the contrasts between
moments of song and moments of dialogue, but also to make those
contrasts especially vivid within the songs themselves where the
sentiments implied by the words could be augmented by, or made
to seem at odds with, the spirit of the music.

The music of the twentieth century had seen an almost complete
break with the symphonic forms and conventions which had
dominated Western music since the eighteenth century and the
work of J.S. Bach (who died in 1750). Just as Picasso brought
about a revolution in the world of painting, to the extent that he
redefined the whole genre, so Schoenberg revolutionised concepts
of music by inventing an entirely new world of atonal sounds,
breaking the accepted relationship between melody, harmony and
counterpoint. While Weill appreciated the achievements of the
Modernist movement – for example, Berg's *Wozzeck*, which he
recognised as a masterpiece – nevertheless he felt that this kind of
modernist work offered no coherent way forward. He was more
sympathetic to another kind of break with the past which had been
made by Igor Stravinsky. Unlike Schoenberg, Berg and others,
Stravinsky (after the public uproar created by his *Rite of Spring* in
1913) returned to earlier periods of music, including the eighteenth
century, in order to explore the possibilities of recycling its very
disciplined forms in recognisably modernist ways. The aspects of
modernism which he chose to integrate with the baroque were the

seemingly unlikely ones of jazz and popular music, rather than the atonality of Schoenberg – precisely the kind of thing that Weill was trying to do in another context.

Both Weill and Stravinsky were very open to American influences, which tended to be popular rather than classical. Stravinsky had used jazz rhythms in his *Histoire du Soldat (The Soldier's Tale*, 1918), which combined music and speech in ways which influenced Weill directly. 'What Stravinsky attempts in his *Soldier's Tale*', he declared in January 1926, 'can count as the mixed genre [*Zwischengattung*] most assured of a future … perhaps it can form the basis of a certain type of new opera' (cited in Hinton, p.182). As Hinton suggests, 'There is much in the Weill-Brecht work – the economy of forces, the visibility of the instrumentalists, the use of modern dance idioms, the epic structure, the separation of elements, the ironic humour – that can be traced back to Stravinsky's pioneering piece of music-theatre.'

The Austrian composer Ernst Krenek also revealed jazz influences in his opera *Jonny spielt auf* (1925–6). The American George Gershwin had managed to integrate the popular and the classical to noteworthy effect and acclaim in his *Rhapsody in Blue* (1924), which was among the first works to combine jazz with symphonic features. A work such as Hindemith's *Cardillac* (1926) may also have been influential in that it introduces a 'distancing' or 'alienation' effect by writing music that progresses in parallel to the text, commenting on the action rather than emphasising its meaning. It was Hindemith who promulgated the idea of 'Gebrauchsmusik' (utility music) – the concept of music as a socially useful activity rather than a rarified phenomenon confined to expensive opera houses. As Weill noted about *The Threepenny Opera*, 'This return to a primitive operatic form entailed a drastic simplification of musical language. It meant writing a kind of music that would be singable by actors, in other words by musical amateurs […] Nothing but the introduction of approachable,

catchy tunes made possible *The Threepenny Opera's* real
achievement: the creation of a new type of musical theatre' (see his
note on pp.89–90 of the present edition).

According to the music critic Hans Keller this was 'the
weightiest possible lowbrow opera for highbrows and the most
full-blooded highbrow musical for lowbrows' (cited in Hinton,
p.146). 'Through-composed' music in the manner of Wagner was
replaced by the principle of musical 'numbers' which shunned the
more earnest traditions of the opera house and created a mixed
form incorporating spoken theatre and popular musical idioms. Or
as another critic, David Drew, suggested:

> In *The Threepenny Opera*, as in *Happy End* [a slightly later Brecht/
> Weill collaboration], every number, however small, is a memorable and
> indeed inspired composition. But what distinguishes *The Threepenny
> Opera* score from its successor are the interacting relationships and
> tensions that combine to create a music-dramatic form. It is the total
> form, and not the quality of the individual numbers, that ultimately
> raises the score to the level of a minor masterpiece.
>
> (Ibid., p.160)

The effect produced by the success of *The Threepenny Opera* was
such that it proved unsettling for someone like Alban Berg, whose
operas *Wozzeck* and *Lulu* had been influenced by Schoenberg's
atonal principles. Two months after the premiere he declared that
'even the likes of us cannot make up their minds in favour of a
"Drei-Groschen-Oper" or a "Zehntausend-Dollar-Symphonie" [a
ten-thousand-dollar symphony]' (ibid., p.187). Berg was possibly
contrasting in his mind the scale of the second and third
symphonies of someone like Gustav Mahler, and the resources
required to perform them, compared with the modest proportions
and expenditure involved in writing and performing an opera in the
style of Weill.

'*The Threepenny Opera*'

The opera opens with an overture which parodies Handelian pomp,
the score marked to be played '*tempo maestoso*' (i.e. majestically).
It is followed by the ballad-singer's 'Moritat' ('The Ballad of Mac
the Knife'). The first thing to note about the opening ballad is its
instrumental scoring and its 'blues' tempo. Instead of an operatic
orchestration, a pianist-director leads a group of eight musicians
who command a range of instruments including two saxophones, a
banjo, a guitar and a bandoneon (a small accordion). The ballad-
singer's introductory presentation is done in a droning fashion 'like
a barrel organ'. Brecht's own recording of the song emphasises the
guttural sound of the German consonants, especially the way in
which the 'r's are rolled. In this ballad, according to Walter
Weideli, the singer

> denounces, by means of brutal contrast, the duplicity of the sharks
> whose murders are accomplished beneath a veneer of elegance and
> respectability. The melody [...] expresses the resignation of whoever
> gives up trying to understand and, therefore, to act. This resignation is
> mixed with vulgar irony and mean joy as if Mackie, the knife-artist,
> were assuming the repressed revolt of all those 'who remain in the
> shadows'. [...] In a way, Brecht lends his voice to the pre-Hitlerian
> demons, but it is in order to subject them to the judgement of his
> conscience. Berlin's sophisticated postwar [i.e. post-First World War]
> audience was deceived. Easily assimilating Brecht's aggressiveness, they
> were unaware of his critical intentions and whisked away his irony.
>
> (Walter Weideli, *The Art of Bertolt Brecht*, London, Merlin Press,
> 1963, pp.26–7)

David Drew in his article 'Motifs, Tags and Related Matters'
(Hinton, pp.149–60) offers a complex musical analysis of the
opening ballad and points to the ways in which the themes in the
opera are connected through the songs. The opening three-note
motif of 'The Ballad of Mac the Knife' is related to Mac's 'Ballad
of the Good Life' and is then inverted by Peachum in his 'Song of

the Insufficiency of Human Endeavour' which is in C major. In its
minor form the notes recur throughout the opera rather like a
leitmotif. In Act Two a 'motto chord' derived from the same three
notes can be identified in tango rhythm which then relates to
Pirate Jenny's whispered warnings in her song and their explosive
variation in the finale to Act One.

Peachum's 'Morning Hymn' is a maudlin dirge sung *'feierlich'*
(solemnly) to organ accompaniment which, in the German original,
makes great play with the guttural effects as in, 'Verschacher dein
Ehweib, du Wicht!' (And sell your old woman, you rat!). This was
the only melody which Weill retained from the original *Beggar's
Opera* but his minimal orchestration differs markedly from
Pepusch's. 'The "No They Can't" Song' is sung to a jaunty
marching rhythm underlined by a solo saxophone. It introduces the
moon motif which is taken up in subsequent songs. In Michel
Perez's words, 'We very quickly identify the moon over Soho that
gazes upon Polly Peachum and Mack's love affairs: it is the same
ill-omened heavenly body which slowly leads Wozzeck [in the
penultimate scene of Berg's opera *Wozzeck* in which the
eponymous anti-hero commits suicide by drowning] into the
middle of its bloody gleam. It is the gilded paper glued to the sky
of Berlin's 'dives', which all of a sudden becomes the star of death,
hanging, like the most wretched and the most disquieting of theatre
accessories, above a field of bleakness.'*

The 'Wedding Song for the Less Well-Off' takes the form of
an all-male 'chorale' (sung *a cappella,* i.e. like a chapel choir) in a
laborious style to rather ponderous rhythms and punctuated by
feeble, unaccompanied exclamations of 'Hooray!', and 'The Swine'
at the end of the choruses. The following song which Polly sings

---

* From a CD booklet to the 1958 recording by the Sender Freies Berlin Orchestra
(with Lotte Lenya as Jenny) conducted by Wilhelm Brückner-Rüggeberg, CBS Inc.,
1982. We have used this recording as a model to characterise the nature of the music
throughout.

about 'Pirate Jenny' (*allegretto*, i.e. in brisk tempo) was one subsequently made popular by Lotte Lenya and is one of the best-known songs from the opera. It opens with long rhythmical phrases accompanied by a noisy piano, before developing a mood of romantic and cruel ecstasy accompanied by the organ. The jog-trotting rhythms of the song contradict the uncomfortable nature of its sentiments although the final three lines of each verse are accompanied by a change of tempo to something altogether more dream-like and menacing. The song represents the fantasy of an exploited and downtrodden barmaid who seeks revenge on the human race, and men in particular, in essentially personal and sexual terms. Her romantic individualism is expressed in terms of false social values which are the only ones its victims can imagine. The mood of the song is most terrifying in the final verse, when the music inserts a pause before 'the lot!' and 'hoppla!'. Pirate Jenny's sense of satisfaction at the sight of the executioner's block is not unrelated to Lucy and Polly's feelings at the sight of the gallows in Scene Nine. She is the dream-like heroine of her own dream-like fantasy – the kind of individual for whom Hollywood subsequently became the dream factory for suppressed desires and wish-fulfilments.

'The Cannon Song' (foxtrot tempo) gains its effects from setting its theme of colonial slaughter to the ragtime rhythms reminiscent of German nightclub music. It owes an obvious debt to Rudyard Kipling's 'Soldiers Three', which became the basis of Brecht's own 'Ballad of the Three Soldiers', as well as to Kipling's poem 'Screw-Guns' with its characteristic sentiment, 'If a man doesn't work, why we drills 'im an' teaches 'im 'ow to behave. / If a beggar can't march, why, we kills 'im an' rattles 'im into 'is grave'. After an upbeat musical introduction, the music settles into a marching rhythm while the words are declaimed raucously and with relish. The change of mood which is evident in the third verse is signalled by a drum roll and a slight *rallentando* (slowing down) before the final chorus, as if gearing up for yet another round of recruitment and violence in an endlessly repetitive cycle. The contrasting love duet, which concludes Scene Two, is important as it concerns a major theme of the opera as a whole. Weideli suggests that

> The conventionally lyrical, and yet heartrending words that [Macheath] exchanges with Polly after her brief wedding night are based on a misunderstanding. Both agree, while playing the dupes during an instant of exhilaration, but even while they are singing their unanimity, Brecht and Weill are reminding us with cruel irony of the secret division by which all love is cursed.
>
> (Op. cit., p.28)

Polly's song to her parents, which follows, about her marriage to Macheath (*moderato assai*, i.e. a very moderate tempo), is about innocence and experience as sung by a sexual tease. In the first two verses Polly describes how she deliberately led men on with no intention of becoming committed and with every intention of rejecting each one. The teasing nature of the song is best illustrated in the measured deliberation of lines 5–9 of each verse where the tempo is reined back slightly and a note of calculation enters the delivery of the words. The third verse effectively reverses the negative terms of the first two without any alteration to the basic mood and rhythm. It is not as if passion has supplanted calculation but that calculation has at last found the target of its desires.

The First *Threepenny* Finale, 'Concerning the Insecurity of the Human Condition', which follows, is one of the most rhythmically varied in the opera. It begins in a brisk march rhythm with words sung in a high-pitched, rather naive voice, by Polly, before adopting a funereal tempo, to organ accompaniment for the next lines, sung by Peachum. Suddenly, however, his last four lines, which clinch the negative sentiments of the song as a whole, are delivered in an upbeat tempo as if the pessimism is being relished by the formerly lugubriously-toned singer. This mood is continued

by Mrs Peachum but resumes its funereal quality for Peachum's
next five lines. However, just as the mood becomes dejected – with
the line, 'But sadly on this planet ... ' – the music reassumes its
jauntiness and the couplet of Polly and Mrs Peachum is given a
positively celebratory feel, despite its apparently pessimistic
conclusion. The remaining lines of the song continue in rapid
tempo, delivered with staccato emphasis and with positively gay
abandon, as if these three find a degree of satisfaction in their final
declaration that, 'The world is poor and man's a shit'. The
orchestral *tutti* (played by the entire musical ensemble) at the end
underscores the staccato and rapid delivery of the singers in a final
rhetorical flourish.

'The Ballad of Sexual Obsession' (*andante quasi largo*, i.e. fairly
slow, broad and dignified) in Act Two is sung in a deliberately
measured, almost breathless *cantilena* (lyrically smooth) style and
its extended delivery is possibly more like a genuine ballad than
many so-called ballads in the opera as a whole. However, its
romantic content is deliberately undercut by its cynical sentiment,
which simply reduces love to appetite as higher aims are seen
consistently to be undermined by lower animal promptings. The
final verse encapsulates the reduction of 'high' to 'low' with
particular force in the German version, where 'oben' is juxtaposed
with the rhyming 'droben'. 'The Ballad of Immoral Earnings'
(tango tempo), which follows, is a coarse anti-romantic romance
where the feel of the music is at odds with the sense of the words.
As Weill observed, 'The charm of the piece rests precisely in the
fact that a rather risqué text [...] is set to music in a gentle
pleasant way' (Hinton, p.188). It amounts to a deliberately
unsettling mixture of sentimentality and caustic social criticism.

The irony of the 'Ballade of Good Living' stems from the fact
that Macheath delivers the song from his prison cell, decrying
freedom if it entails poverty, and advocating a complacent, well-
heeled, bourgeois existence which denigrates both intellectual and

physical effort, turns its back on human misery and derides any sense of historical perspective or relativity. The first four lines of each verse are sung in a jaunty, jazzy, carefree style with a banal two-note punctuation on the piano at the end of each line. But then the listener becomes aware that the underlying accompaniment to lines 5 to 8 is reminiscent of the previous song, 'The Ballad of Immoral Earnings'. The tempo slows for line 9, which becomes a precise echo of the line in the earlier number about 'the whorehouse where we used to live', and which is then repeated, in a slightly faster tempo, for the final line of each verse. The sense of bourgeois comfort which equates happiness and the meaning of life with the acquisition of wealth becomes synonymous with a world made in the image of pimps, whores and their clients.

'The Jealousy Duet' (*tempo agitato*, i.e. restless, or agitated) varies its style as the women spit fire at each other one minute in a rapid exchange of insults, before incongruously uniting in a sentimental duet where they both lay claim to Mac's affections. This brief sentimental alliance, which is in fact rivalry, is re-asserted with the final exclamation, repeated at the end of the song: 'Poppycock' (in the original 'Lächerlich!' (Laughable!)). The opening verse with its repetitious rhythms sounds like a standard cabaret number and with interventions by Polly spoken rather than sung. The single line exchanges are then delivered very rapidly in a form of 'Sprechgesang' (or 'spoken song').

The Second *Threepenny* Finale, 'What Keeps Mankind Alive', is divided into parts – a fact not reflected in the present text but apparent in the original. Macheath sings the first ten lines which are followed by an offstage chorus asking, 'What keeps mankind alive?', which Macheath then answers in the next three-and-a-half lines with the chorus taking up the last two. The pattern is repeated for the second verse but with Jenny singing the lines which Macheath sang in the first. The opening ten lines of both verses are sung to a slow march rhythm reminiscent of a New

Orleans street funeral band but with the answer to the question, 'What keeps mankind alive?', sung in a livelier tempo belying the accompanying sentiments of the words. The final two lines of each verse sung by the chorus are delivered in a solemn and declamatory fashion that would seem to brook no argument.

Next, the 'Song of the Insufficiency of Human Endeavour' is sung to an almost light-hearted, jazzy rhythm. The melody repeated in the first two lines of each verse and the syncopated beat in the last line of each stanza emphasise a certain carefree cheekiness about mankind's inadequacies which form the song's subject. This is immediately followed by the 'Solomon Song', sung to a rocking rhythm provided by a small accordion and to a melody not unlike that of 'The Wild Colonial Boy'.

David Drew describes the final musical episodes of *The Threepenny Opera* as follows:

> Macheath's suffering is the wholly serious subject of the two numbers which follow the 'Salamon-Song' [he gives the German spelling] . . . . Weill's superb setting of the 'Epistel' culminates in a furiously denunciatory passage [. . .] Macheath is no longer the engaging rogue of the previous scenes, indeed, is no longer Macheath. He has become a tragic figure who speaks with the voice of all whom the world, justly or unjustly, has condemned. It is a voice that cries for vengeance as loudly as for forgiveness. [. . .] Weill was not exaggerating when he claimed for the finale a relationship to opera in its 'purest, most pristine form'.
>
> (Cited in Hinton, pp.155-7)

At this point the *deus ex machina* parodies traditional opera with a pastiche of a Lutheran hymn as the chorus warns against trying to overcome injustice and, in so doing, echoes the moralising hymn-tune at the end of many cantatas by J.S. Bach. 'Rob not the poor, neither oppress the afflicted', says the biblical Book of Proverbs, which goes on to maintain that the Lord will plead their cause.

The chorus, on the other hand, states that injustice should be allowed to perish of its own accord, with the presumption that the poor will have perished from the cold long before injustice does. Brecht would seem to be implying that the poor had better intervene on their own behalf, otherwise they are going to have to wait an eternity.

Performance history

German productions

The original production at the Theater am Schiffbauerdamm in Berlin, directed by Erich Engel, opened on 31 August 1928, and ran for more than 350 performances over the next two years. Probably because of its English connections with Gay and Kipling, a correspondent of *The Times* newspaper went to see the production and filed a report which appeared in the paper on 25 September under the heading '*The Threepenny Opera*: A Berlin Burlesque':

> There is a piece being played at the Theater am Schiffbauerdamm, in Berlin, called *Die Dreigroschenoper* (*The Threepenny Opera*). An English visitor who omitted to buy the inadequate programme generally provided in Berlin theatres, or paid very slight attention to it, would wonder, during the first scene, what it was all about. He would conclude that he had blundered into one of those combinations of drama, cinema, jazz and discord with which the name of the Communistic Herr Piscator is associated. He would, perhaps, have even been more bewildered if he had noticed beforehand in small letters beneath the title '*The Beggar's Opera* a piece with music, in prologue and eight scenes, after the English of John Gay, with ballads by François Villon and Rudyard Kipling inserted'.
>
> Gradually something familiar would strike him, rather in general than in detail; then he would learn, from cinematograph captions flashed on

the wings in the best Piscatorial manner, that the formal name of Mackie Messer, the bandit chief in the bowler hat, was Captain Macheath, and other well-known names, such as Peachum, Polly, and Lucy, would become distinguishable. At first, like the loyal Savoyard [an enthusiast for the operettas of Gilbert and Sullivan] at last year's German production of *The Mikado* as a *revue*, he might feel indignant; at the close he might well conclude that, although what he had seen was not *The Beggar's Opera*, it retained in some accountable way, the spirit in which John Gay burlesqued the manners, the morals, and grand opera of his day, and provided a good evening's entertainment. He might even, like the enthusiasts of the last London revival [at the Lyric Theatre, Hammersmith, in 1920] want to go again.

What Herr Brecht and his associates have done may be indefensible to many minds but it is an interesting example of the more earnest efforts now being made to break new ground on the German stage. Herr Brecht, in his adaptation, starts from the standpoint that *The Beggar's Opera* is a bright idea, with a good story pervaded with fun and satire, that, as it was written partly as a skit on a form of grand opera that no longer cries for drastic chastisement, he decided to reduce that element, which only remains in its full original absurdity in the last scene. As, too, Gay made use only of popular airs of the day, it was decided to provide entirely new music. The absence of any of the Old English airs is regrettable, but the music composed by Herr Kurt Weill for the Lewis Ruth Jazz Band is by no means unattractive ... [The Lewis Ruth Band, a seven-man outfit of versatile jazz studio musicians (named after the band's flautist and saxophonist Ludwig Rüth) provided the instrumental accompaniment. Theo Mackeben directed from the piano.]

Having discarded much of the opera burlesque and all of the music, there apparently seemed no reason for retaining the eighteenth-century atmosphere, so Herr Brecht put the scene forward, not 200 years, but about 170. It is vaguely about the end of the nineteenth century, a period which provides picturesque and convincing costumes and make-ups for Peachum and his beggars, though it has led to a temptation to present Macheath's 'street bandits' as music-hall tramps of the present day. Macheath himself wears a bowler hat of old style, a large white pointed collar, a double-breasted blue lounge suit with black silk lapels and tight trousers. He carries a yellow cane and generally gives the impression of a fourth-rate professional boxer. Herr Harald Paulsen, however, almost succeeds in giving him the devil-may-care personality of Macheath. Herr Erich Ponto's Jonathan Peachum is an excellent performance.

The production of the piece is deliberately crude. Adopting the idea that it should be a 'Threepenny Opera', which fits in well with tendencies now in the dramatic air, the producers have provided a dirty cream-coloured curtain about 10ft high, worked by a primitive arrangement of strings, such as might be used in amateur theatricals. Across the curtain is painted in crooked, badly-formed letters, 'Die Dreigroschenoper'. For the stable scene, in which Macheath and Polly celebrate their wedding breakfast, there is provided only a wooden wall a few feet high and a door. The rest of the stable is indicated by means of the cinematograph. There is an occasionally expressionistic touch, such as the sudden letting-down of a placard by ropes from above.

There are regrettable omissions, such as the appearance at the execution of Macheath's former loves with their babies, and some doubt may be expressed as to whether such *revue*-like additions as the brothel scene, in which Macheath is arrested, are really in the spirit of John Gay. The ballads after Villon and – so it is said, though one failed to identify them – Mr Kipling, sung by Peachum and Macheath, almost give the piece at times the air, deliberately fostered by music and effects, of a morality play [sixteenth-century didactic plays with abstract characters, on subjects of a moral nature]. But *Die Dreigroschenoper* is not, of course, a morality play, it is not a *revue*, it is not a conventional burlesque, and it is not *The Beggar's Opera*; but it is an interesting combination of them illustrating the progress of a movement towards freeing music, acting, and the cinematograph from the ruts of Italian opera, Wagnerian music-drama, drawing-room comedy, and Hollywood, and creating something new with them.

The Austrian novelist and essayist, Elias Canetti, who lived in Berlin at the time, saw the production and wondered about the audience's reaction. If the play was designed to anatomise the bourgeoisie, ought the audience of well-heeled respectable Berliners to have been quite so pleased with what they saw?

> It was a stylish production, coolly calculated. It was the most precise expression of Berlin. The people cheered themselves, they saw themselves, and were pleased. First came *their* food, then came their morality, no-one could have put it better, they took it literally. Now it had been said, no bug in a rug could have felt snugger. [...] Only those who experienced it can believe the grating and bare self-satisfaction that emanated from this production. [...] What one had done was to take the saccharine form of Viennese operetta, in which people found their wishes undisturbed, and oppose it with a Berlin form, with its hardness, meanness and banal justifications, which people wanted no less, probably even more, than all that sweetness.
>
> (Quoted in Hinton, pp. 190–2)

The theatre critic Herbert Jhering thought the play and the production succeeded in erasing the boundaries between tragedy and comedy. It was a triumph of open form. Another critic sensed this dissolution of traditional theatrical categories into 'something new that is all things at once: irony and symbol, grotesque and protest, opera and popular melody; an attempt which gives subversion the last word and which, leaving its theatrical claims aside, could represent an important phase in the otherwise directionless discussion about the form of the revue' (ibid., p.56). A communist critic, on the other hand, thought there was no trace of modern social or political satire in it; it was an 'entertaining mishmash', while the critic of a right-wing newspaper recommended the production to anyone suffering from sleeplessness as he 'quietly fell asleep after the first five minutes' and so was, 'unfortunately unable to say anything about the content of the piece' (ibid., pp.56–7).

Within a year the play had been performed 4,200 times in some 120 theatres. Within three years, eighteen recordings in eighteen languages had been issued. 'Threepenny fever' gripped everyone, with the tunes being whistled in the street and a 'Threepenny Opera Bar' opening in which only tunes from the show were played. A twenty-four-page edition of the songs was published in October 1928 in a print-run of 10,000 copies which was reprinted early the following year and, shortly afterwards, a third print-run of between sixteen and twenty thousand was made. With the arrival of the Nazis, the play was banned and did not receive another German production until after the war when, unbeknown to Brecht, it was staged at the Hebbel Theatre in Berlin in July 1945. As James K. Lyon points out, the success of the production rather embarrassed Brecht when he found out about it, given that the state of the German population at the time was not dissimilar to that of real, rather than sham, beggars, and the sentiment 'Eats first; morals later' might have communicated the wrong idea to an impoverished people:

Hungry Berliners subsisting on a food ration of one loaf of bread and a quarter of a pound of butter per month and a quarter-pound of meat per week (cheese, milk, sugar, salt and coffee were virtually unobtainable) found in it a welcome form of protest against the occupying powers who wanted to de-Nazify them without feeding them properly. Robert Joseph, a United States Army film officer in Berlin [. . .] describes the postwar première [. . .]: 'The people loved the show [. . .] and when Mackie sings the song "Zuerst Fressen, danach Moral" [Eats first; morals later] they applauded madly. [. . .] The Russians have decided, as of last evening, that they don't like the show. They think that song is inciting, and I think they'll insist on closing it.' [. . .] Brecht's journal notes that he agrees with the Russians [. . .] 'In

the absence of a revolutionary movement, the "message" is pure
anarchy.'

(James K. Lyon, *Bertolt Brecht in America,* London, Methuen, 1982,
pp.310–11)

The next production was staged at the Kammerspiele Theatre,
Munich, in April 1949, directed by Harry Buckwitz and employing
the play's original designer, Brecht's childhood friend and
colleague, Caspar Neher. By this stage Germany was a divided
nation, with Brecht residing in the Russian sector of East Berlin
and staging his own plays with his own company, the Berliner
Ensemble, who had taken over the Theater am Schiffbauerdamm
where the first production of *The Threepenny Opera* had been
staged. In what had become West Germany, a production was
mounted in Cologne in 1961. An East German critic thought it
was scandalous:

The show was a mixture of Anouilh [a contemporary French dramatist
with a penchant for recycling myth], Ionesco [one of the leading
representatives of 'The Theatre of the Absurd'], *West Side Story* and
Cologne carnival. Mac the Knife in a red dinner jacket and with an
existentialist's beard. Polly [...] appeared on stage in a long evening
dress or in ultra-elegant trousers shot with gold. The beggar king
Peachum in his black dinner suit looked like the director of a West
German conglomerate ... Tap dancing during the scene shifts;
stagehands vacuum up non-existent dust [...]. The whores were
charming call girls who advertised Dralon underwear. The text was
mutilated and supplemented quite arbitrarily.

(Cited in Hinton, pp.59–60)

Harry Buckwitz made another attempt at staging the play in
Frankfurt-am-Main, West Germany, in April 1965, on this occasion
employing the services of another of Brecht's designers, Teo Otto.
According to the *Frankfurter Allgemeine Zeitung,*

Buckwitz has started out with Brecht's remarks that this is an opera for

beggars. As the curtain rose you saw the entire cast grouped in front of
a raised stage in a grey London back yard. Squatting along the
footlights, standing at the sides, was a pauper public audience for a show
that was about to start. The theatre's own audience was its continuation.

(*Bertolt Brecht on Stage*, Bad Godesberg, Inter Nationes, 1968)

The attempt to enforce the 'distancing' effect by means of the
device of the audience watching another audience watching the play
seems to have misunderstood Brecht's sense of what an 'opera for
beggars' meant. During the 1974/75 season another production was
mounted in the West German town of Düsseldorf, set in
contemporay times, with Mac in a pin-striped suit and Peachum as
an elegant businessman. Instead of a brothel, Mac visited a massage
parlour and, in order to enhance the social criticism, passages from
Brecht's *The Threepenny Novel* were incorporated and the ending
changed. Just as Macheath was about to be hanged, Brown
informed Peachum that Macheath was in possession of some very
valuable stocks and shares, whereupon Peachum demanded he be
released and welcomed him as his son-in-law. Together they
established the Peachum-Brown-Macheath Company.

The Berliner Ensemble did not revive the play until April 1960,
approximately four years after Brecht's death. It was again directed
by the, now ageing, Erich Engel and was performed on 342
occasions until the end of the 1964/5 season. It was seen in Prague,
Budapest and, in 1965, in London where the Ensemble had toured
for the first time in 1956. In 1965, the group also brought to
London productions of Brecht's plays, *Coriolan, The Resistible Rise
of Arturo Ui* and *Days of the Commune.* Critics were stunned by
the first two, impressed by the third, but remained cool about *The
Threepenny Opera.* David Drew best sums up the qualities of a
production which seemed to have been tailored to cause little
offence to foreign audiences during a period of thaw in the on-
going Cold War between the Western and Eastern bloc countries.
Drew was especially disappointed with the music:

In this version which the Ensemble is now presenting at the Old Vic, the entire accompanimental texture of Weill's score has been turned inside out. Whereas it should be dominated by the wind instruments and backed by piano, plucked instruments and percussion, here it is dominated by a spurious rhythm section – treated in the manner of a provincial night-club band of the late Fifties – and backed by the remnants of the original texture, from which many of the threads are missing. The *sostenuto* and *legato* characters, which convey the very essence of Weill's minatory lyricism are obliterated, and the autonomy of the *commenting* accompaniment is further undermined by futile improvisations and gratuitous doublings of the voice parts – more often than not by an (over-) amplified guitar, which is not specified by Weill, and which is as appropriate to this sound-picture as a splash of luminous paint on a pencil drawing [...] It is significant that the one number that really comes off – the 'Jealousy Duet', beautifully done by Annemone Haase and Christine Gloger – has been left more or less as Weill composed it, and is musically simple. For the most part phrasing, in the musical sense, is either non-existent, or else so exaggerated for parodistic purposes as to be deprived of any inherent value. [...] Formally, the score remains more or less intact up to the third and last finale, which is by rights the culmination. In the second of the finale's two main sections, the whole work should acquire a new dimension. The Berliner Ensemble remove this second section, having previously used the Peachums' march duet, in an abominable arrangement for orchestra alone, as incidental music (a convention wholly foreign to the work). The production closes, not with the synoptic chorale, but with a raucous pop version of the Moritat.

(David Drew, 'Demonstrations', *New Statesman*, 20 August 1965, pp.262–4)

The American critic, Robert Brustein, shared some of David Drew's disappointment:

[...] this version lacks pace, integration or coherence [...] The style is relatively realistic, modified by vestigial alienation techniques (the orchestra, for example, is placed on an upstage platform behind a curtain which parts at the beginning of each song). Wolf Kaiser plays Mackie Messer [...] as a suave, thickening, middle-aged Lothario – brutish and dapper, with the heavy grace of an aging dancer and the sad lethargy of a basset hound. [...] At Mackie's wedding to Polly [...] he kicks his henchman in the behind at the same moment a champagne cork pops; implored by Polly to stay and make love to her, he curtly refuses – but stops for one searching look at her legs; when he sits down to his account books, he puts on the rimless glasses of a serious businessman.

(Robert Brustein, *The Third Theatre*, London, Jonathan Cape, 1970, p.136)

The play was revived again by the Berliner Ensemble in 1985, directed by Manfred Wekwerth and with Stefan Lisewski as Macheath.

The 1986/87 statistics for new theatrical productions in West Germany placed Brecht's play alongside *Hamlet* in seventh position, with both plays receiving ten new stagings in one season. However, in terms of audience figures, *The Threepenny Opera* was top of the list, attracting approximately 174,000 people – that is, twice as many as the Shakespeare play.

British productions

Apart from *The Times* review of the first German production (already quoted), the *Illustrated London News* reported a production of what it called 'The Threefarthings Opera' [a farthing being one quarter of an old penny], staged in Darmstadt on 23 November 1929, which it described as 'a very curious version of *The Beggar's Opera*'. In February 1935, the BBC broadcast *The Tuppeny-ha'penny Opera* [two-and-a-half pence being a ha'penny (half a penny) short of three old pence] as 'an opera specially written for beggars'. Weill himself described it in a letter as 'the worst performance imaginable'. It was reviewed in the *Sunday Times* by the famous music critic Ernest Newman who described it as 'beggarly':

> The 'Dreigroschen Oper' of Bert Brecht (text) and Kurt Weill (music) [...] is described by its authors as 'after *The Beggar's Opera* of John Gay'. It may be after that masterpiece, but it will certainly never catch up with it: these two dull dogs achieve the almost incredible feat of making even crime boring. It is difficult to say which is feebler, the libretto or the music – perhaps the latter, which has the worst faults of more than one bad style and the qualities of not a single good one, even at second hand.

After these undistinguished beginnings, matters could only improve. In February of the year in which the Berliner Ensemble came to London for the first time, 1956, Sam Wanamaker directed *The Threepenny Opera* at the Royal Court Theatre, London, with the folk-singer Ewan MacColl as the ballad singer (he had been connected with Joan Littlewood and left-wing street theatre before the war). The young Warren Mitchell was a member of Macheath's gang and the sadly miscast Bill Owen was Macheath. Musical direction was in the hands of Berthold Goldschmidt, a distinguished composer in his own right as well as someone, like Brecht, who had been forced to flee Nazi Germany. The doyen of English theatre critics of the time and, later, a Brecht enthusiast, Kenneth Tynan, described the production as retaining Caspar Neher's scenery, plus the use of signs and lantern slides and forgave the production its shortcomings. This was a musical show in which there were at least no life-denying lies, 'no word or note is coy, dainty or sugary', and in which 'Brecht's honesty, tart though it tastes, is an affirmation. It says that whoever we are, and however vile, we are worth singing about' (*Observer*, 12 February 1956).

A production by Tony Richardson, better known as a film director, opened in April 1972 at the Prince of Wales Theatre, with his wife, Vanessa Redgrave, as Polly. A translation had been

specially prepared for this production by the Scots nationalist poet
and communist, Hugh MacDiarmid. Barbara Windsor (then a star
of the *Carry On . . .* films) introduced what was described as a
slightly discordant note to the role of Lucy. Hermione Baddeley
was a gin-soaked Mrs Peachum straight out of *The Beggar's Opera*.
Critics, generally, were unenthusiastic. The production seemed too
full of star turns and incongruities, with Vanessa Redgrave's Polly
having 'strayed from a Wimbledon garden party', according to the
theatre critic of the *Evening Standard*.

In 1978, director and designer at the Glasgow Citizens Theatre,
Philip Prowse, staged a production for Opera North. It began with
a group of tramps, who might have escaped from a film by the
Spanish surrealist Luis Buñuel, breaking into the salon of a
mansion in Belgravia. The set was decorated in pink and powder-
blue with an ornately painted ceiling, elaborate chandelier, and a
grand piano being played by a bored elderly dowager who turned
out to be a man in women's clothing. The tramps proceeded to
present 'her' with a performance of the opera, enlisting her butler
as Macheath and the maids as Jenny, Lucy, and a 'punk' Polly, and
with the gang doubling as whores in drag. Mrs Peachum was acted
as an alcoholic pushing a pram containing nothing but a bottle of
gin. At the end of the performance, which the dowager was forced
to watch while tied to a chair, the tramps slit her throat. At one
point, the top of the grand piano was made to double as
Macheath's prison cell and the rope to hang him was slung from
the chandelier. According to *The Times* it was more like Stanley
Kubrick's film of Anthony Burgess's *A Clockwork Orange* than
the Brecht/Weill work, although 'it is sometimes a closer
approximation of Brecht's Germanic England than many a more
dutiful production' (2 October 1978).

A production by Peter Wood was staged at the National Theatre
in 1986, in yet another new version – this time by Philip Prowse's
co-director at the Glasgow Citizens Theatre, Robert David

MacDonald, with Dominic Muldowney as musical director and
Tim Curry as a foppish Macheath. Michael Billington considered it
a bland, smooth and pretty production, 'where the only irony is
that the show is sponsored by Citicorps and Citibank' (*One Night
Stands*, London, Nick Hern Books, 1993, p.253). It was 'a pleasant
bourgeois spectacle' which began with a black-plumed funeral
cortege. 'The real passions in this production seem to be
decorative, from the swivelling round of the Turnbridge
whorehouse set for a smoke-filled rooftop chase of Macheath to
the sporting of canine masks by the Victorian rozzers.' For
Sheridan Morley it all looked too much like 'a guest night in
Highgate Cemetery' – a reference possibly prompted by its being
the final resting place of Karl Marx, among others (*Our Theatre in
the Eighties*, London, Hodder & Stoughton, 1990, pp.133–4).

A Brecht centenary production was staged at the Playhouse,
Newcastle-upon-Tyne, in 1998, directed by Neil Murray, using
Robert David MacDonald's translation and with new lyrics by
Jeremy Sams, with one rewritten line suggesting that, 'If you think
poverty romantic, pack your bags and live in Ethiopia'. According
to Sean O'Brien, the production 'report[ed] on a distant outrage to
an audience which cannot be shocked by poverty, scandalised or
thrilled by sexual display, or led to think of itself in relation to the
events depicted, and thus the performance is made to look like part
of the problem it was intended to solve' (*Times Literary
Supplement*, 20 March 1998). The atmosphere of the production
was 'threadbare' and apart from the introduction of a few
swearwords, tame in the extreme: 'So, no danger of a revolution on
the Tyne at present, then. The Cabinet can sleep soundly in their
bondage gear' (ibid.). Taking a leaf out of the Philip Prowse's 1978
production book, Polly Peachum was played as a punk in pink
gingham with Mrs Peachum wearing 'a shock of purple hair' but
otherwise looking 'like a moth-eaten Queen Victoria' (*Guardian*, 24
March 1998). Finally, the messenger descended from heaven

looking like 'a camp, cute cherub in a mass of white and gilt'.

Other productions

Reviewing the play's Austrian premiere in Vienna in 1929, a critic wrote enthusiastically that

> Weill's music is as characteristic as Brecht's language, as electrifying in its rhythm as the lines of the poems, as deliberately and triumphantly trivial and full of allusions as the popularizing rhymes, as witty in the jazz treatment of the instruments, as contemporary, high-spirited and full of mood and aggression, as the text.
>
> (Cited in Hinton, p.188)

It was the Soviet Minister of Culture, Anatoli Lunacharsky, who first brought Russia's attention to *The Threepenny Opera,* which he had seen while in Berlin during 1929. When Brecht visited Russia during the 1930s he was able to see the production staged by Aleksandr Tairov at his Kamerny Theatre in 1930 as *The Beggars' Opera* (Opera nishchikh). At the time, Brecht was unpublished in the Soviet Union and did not become more widely known until the mid-1930s, largely through the efforts of Sergei Tretiakov. The production was staged as a tragi-farce with décor by the Stenberg brothers who provided a central device of screens and doors, used very effectively in the brothel scenes, which were staged on a revolving carousel which revealed a girl in various stages of undress behind each door. The play was acted in a satirically grotesque, pamphleteering style as the exaggerated and eccentric nature of the characters sought to expose the cynicism and corruption of a mercantile society. The anti-capitalist emphasis was certainly something which Soviet officialdom demanded and critics tended to approve of it despite a certain expressionistic colouring in the production as a whole. It had at least managed to overcome what was seen to be one of the main dangers, i.e.

'render heroic or romanticise the "bandit-vagrant" elements in the
play' (Nick Worrall, *From Modernism to Realism on the Soviet
Stage*, Cambridge University Press, 1989, p.54). Brecht seems to
have been impressed by the way in which, in the first scene,
Peachum's beggars were first seen entering the changing booths as
normal human beings, before leaving them as horrible wrecks.
Although some of Brecht's plays were published in Tretiakov's
Russian translation during the 1930s, none was staged during the
remainder of Stalin's reign and Tretiakov himself was 'purged' in
1937. *The Threepenny Opera* itself was not staged in Russia again
until 1963 when a production was given at the Stanislavsky Theatre
in Moscow.

Probably the most famous production of the play, apart from the
original 1928 version, was the one staged by Giorgio Strehler at the
Piccolo Theatre, Milan, in 1956, which was subsequently revived on
three occasions in 1958, 1960 and 1973. Strehler had gone to Berlin
to meet Brecht in advance of the production in order to ask him
certain questions. Brecht was sufficiently interested to take the
trouble to travel to Milan for the final rehearsals and the premiere
and subsequently stated that the production had been 'brilliant in
conception and detail and very aggressive' (letter of 9 February
1956). A transcript of a conversation between Brecht and Strehler
is included on pp.91–6 of the present volume. The action was set
in 1914 with sets by Teo Otto. The music was also re-orchestrated
to accentuate the jazz element and to enhance the sense of an
Americanised, rather than a British, ambience. As David Hirst has
described it,

> Strehler [...] set the first production in New York, immediately prior
> to the First World War. The concept of American-style gangsters was
> therefore basic [...] Gags from silent-screen comedy abounded: the
> policemen who arrest Macheath were dressed like English bobbies and
> behaved like the Keystone Cops. [...] the scene of Macheath's
> wedding to Polly took place not in a stable but in a garage, the

matrimonial bed for the couple being provided by opening up the back
of a large limousine. Strehler's understanding of the significance of the
Gestus in Brecht's work was evident in sequences where the political
satire is at its sharpest [...] One of these [developed in a later
production] was an invention of Strehler's at the end of the first scene
of Act Three where Peachum's beggars, one after the other, slowly file
across the stage in an increasingly horrific exhibition of distress and
physical disability, all the more disturbing because it was faked.

  (David L. Hirst, *Giorgio Strehler*, Cambridge University Press, 1993,
  p. 98)

As Strehler explained,

  The *Gestus* is not a matter of aesthetics but of social observation. For
  Brecht it has ideological connotations and is meant to disorientate us. ...
  [If someone is miming dumbness] We must be made aware of *how* she
  is miming and *why*; if it's done in one way it's a *Gestus*, if in another it
  might just be mimed dance.

  (Ibid.)

The most memorable American production was the first, staged in
1954 by Marc Blitzstein, which had the distinct advantage of
having Lotte Lenya in the cast who, together with her husband
Kurt Weill, had moved to America in 1935. Although an artistic
failure, it was a resounding commercial success in the wake of
which more than forty 'pop' versions of the Moritat ballad,
marketed as 'Mac the Knife', resulted in ten million pressings, as
well as grossing 10,000,000 dollars for a version recorded by Bobby
Darin in 1959. A later version recorded by Louis Armstrong was
also extremely successful. Latterly, as Philip Brady noted in a
review of Hinton's book of essays on Kurt Weill, 'It took the
admen a long time to realize that, with a character called Mack and
a refrain about Beefsteak Tartar, *The Threepenny Opera* has the
makings of a Big Mac commercial. But in 1987 the truth dawned
and the Ballad of Mac the Knife was relaunched by McDonalds,
with lyrics transformed to celebrate a "Big Mac Tonite"' (*Times*

Literary Supplement).

Writing of the Blitzstein production, the American director and critic, Harold Clurman, thought it a miracle that the inherent superiority of the material managed to survive an otherwise poor performance. This was his conclusion to an extremely perceptive discussion of the significance of the actual play:

> *The Threepenny Opera* is a masterpiece; [so] called [...] because it is so oddly conceived that it might be a beggar's dream and so cheaply done that it might meet a beggar's budget – sums up a whole epoch and evokes a special state of mind. The epoch is not just the Berlin of 1919–28; it is any epoch in which a lurid rascality combined with fierce contrasts of prosperity and poverty shape the dominant tone of society. The state of mind is one of social impotence so close to despair that it expresses itself through a kind of jaded mockery which mingles a snarl with tears. Such in a way was the England of John Gay's *The Beggar's Opera* (1728), from which the Brecht 'book' derives, and certainly the Germany which preceded Hitler. No wonder the one period produced William Hogarth and the other George Grosz. [...] There is, despite the sharp sense of period that permeates it, a universal quality in *The Threepenny Opera*. It fosters a bitter sense of regret that we live so scabbily in relation to our dreams and also a kind of masochistic attachment to our wounds, as if they were all we have to show as evidence of our dreams. [...] How poignant is the sullied lyricism of this work with its jeering bathos, its low-life romanticism, its sweetly poisonous nostalgia, its musical profanity, and its sudden hints of grandeur, godliness, and possible greatness! Here in contemporary terms and with a strange timelessness is the ambiguous, corrupt seduction of a submerged half-world akin to that which François Villon sang of long ago. How disappointing, then, to have as unique a work [...] reduced to a minor event by so ill-prepared a performance.
>
> (Harold Clurman, *The Divine Pastime: Theatre Essays*, New York, Macmillan, 1974, pp.31–2).

Further Reading

Benjamin, Walter, 'Brecht's *Threepenny Novel*, in his *Understanding Brecht*, trs. Anna Bostock, London, New Left Books, 1973

Bentley, Eric, 'The Threepenny Opera', in his *The Brecht Commentaries*, New York, Grove Press, 1987

Brecht, Bertolt, *The Threepenny Opera*, trs. Hugh MacDiarmid, London, Methuen, 1973

Brecht, Bertolt, *The Threepenny Novel*, trs. Desmond I. Vesey, London, Granada, 1981

Brecht, Bertolt, 'The *Threepenny* Material (1930–1932)', in *Brecht on Film and Radio*, trs. and ed. Marc Silberman, London, Methuen, 2001

Ewen, Frederic, *Bertolt Brecht: His Life, His Art & His Times*, London, Calder & Boyars, 1970

Fuegi, John, 'Most Unpleasant Things with *The Threepenny Opera*: Weill, Brecht, and Money', in Kim H. Kowalke (ed.), *A New Orpheus: Essays on Kurt Weill*, New Haven and London, Yale University Press, 1986, pp.157–82

Gay, John, 'The Beggar's Opera', in *The Beggar's Opera and Other Eighteenth Century Plays*, London, J.M. Dent, 1974

Giles, Steve, 'Rewriting Brecht: *Die Dreigroschenoper* 1928–1931', in *Literaturwissenschaftliches Jahrbuch* 30 (1989), pp.249–79

Hinton, Stephen (ed.), *Kurt Weill – 'The Threepenny Opera'*, Cambridge, Cambridge University Press, 1990

Jameson, Fredric, *Brecht and Method*, London, Verso, 1998

Lenya-Weill, Lotte, 'Threepenny Opera', in Hubert Witt (ed.), *Brecht as They Knew Him*, London, Lawrence & Wishart, 1974

McNeff, Stephen, 'The Threepenny Opera', in Peter Thomson and Glendyr Sacks (eds), The Cambridge Companion to Brecht, Cambridge, Cambridge University Press, 1994

Pabst, G.W., The Threepenny Opera, adapted from the musical by B. Brecht and K. Weill, Classic Film Scripts, London, Lorrimer Publishing, 1984 (the scenario of the 1931 film)

Speirs, Ronald, 'A Note on the First Published Version of Die Dreigroschenoper and its Relation to the Standard Text', in Forum for Modern Language Studies 13 (1977), pp.25–32

Villon, François, The Complete Works, trs. Anthony Bonner, New York, Bantam Books, 1960

Völker, Klaus, Brecht: A Biography, trs. John Nowell, London, Marian Boyars, 1979

Weisstein, Ulrich, 'Brecht's Victorian Version of Gay: Imitation and Originality in the Dreigroschenoper', in Comparative Literature Studies 7 (1970), pp.314–35

Willett, John, The Theatre of Bertolt Brecht: A Study From Eight Aspects, London, Methuen, 1959

Willett, John (ed. and trs.), Brecht on Theatre – The Development of an Aesthetic, London, Methuen, 1964

Willett, John, Brecht in Context: Comparative Approaches, London, Methuen, 1984; revised edition, 1998

G.W. Pabst's 1931 film of The Threepenny Opera is available in both a German and French version on a British Film Institute Video (BFIV 025), 1998. The German version features Carola Neher as Polly and Lotte Lenya as Jenny.

The most authentic music for The Threepenny Opera can be heard on a newly-remastered Teldec CD (0927 426632) of a recording made in 1930 with the original cast (apart from the interpreter of Macheath) and with the original Lewis Ruth Band, conducted by Theo Mackeben, together with its strikingly unusual instrumentation. It is not a recording of the complete opera but the thirteen numbers it contains give an excellent idea of how the first production must have sounded. The CD also contains recordings made in 1929 by Brecht himself singing the opening 'Ballad of Mac the Knife' and 'The Song of the Insufficiency of Human Endeavour'.

BBC Radio 3's *Record Review*, broadcast on 6 June 2004, recommended the complete musical version of *The Threepenny Opera* recorded in 1988 by the Berlin RIAS Sinfonietta and Chamber Choir, conducted by John Mauceri, on Decca 430075–2, with René Kollo, Ute Lemper and Helga Dernesch.

All Brecht's major plays (and many minor works) are published by Methuen Drama in English translation in *Brecht: Collected Plays*, vols 1–8. Also published by Methuen Drama are volumes of Brecht's *Journals 1934–1955* and *Brecht on Art and Politics*.

The Threepenny Opera
after John Gay: The Beggar's Opera

Collaborators: ELISABETH HAUPTMANN, KURT WEILL

Translators: RALPH MANHEIM, JOHN WILLETT

Characters
MACHEATH, *called Mac the Knife*
JONATHAN JEREMIAH PEACHUM, *proprietor of the Beggar's Friend Ltd*
CELIA PEACHUM, *his wife*
POLLY PEACHUM, *his daughter*
BROWN, *High Sheriff of London*
LUCY, *his daughter*
LOW-DIVE JENNY
SMITH
THE REVEREND KIMBALL
FILCH
A BALLAD SINGER
THE GANG
Beggars
Whores
Constables

PROLOGUE

The Ballad of Mac the Knife

Fair in Soho.

The beggars are begging, the thieves are stealing, the whores are whoring. A ballad singer sings a ballad.

See the shark with teeth like razors.
All can read his open face.
And Macheath has got a knife, but
Not in such an obvious place.

See the shark, how red his fins are
As he slashes at his prey.
Mac the Knife wears white kid gloves which
Give the minimum away.

By the Thames's turbid waters
Men abruptly tumble down.
Is it plague or is it cholera?
Or a sign Macheath's in town?

On a beautiful blue Sunday
See a corpse stretched in the Strand.
See a man dodge round the corner . . .
Mackie's friends will understand.

And Schmul Meier, reported missing
Like so many wealthy men:
Mac the Knife acquired his cash box.
God alone knows how or when.

Peachum goes walking across the stage from left to right with his wife and daughter.

Jenny Towler turned up lately
With a knife stuck through her breast
While Macheath walks the Embankment
Nonchalantly unimpressed.

Where is Alfred Gleet the cabman?
Who can get that story clear?
All the world may know the answer
Just Macheath has no idea.

And the ghastly fire in Soho –
Seven children at a go –
In the crowd stands Mac the Knife, but he
Isn't asked and doesn't know.

And the child-bride in her nightie
Whose assailant's still at large
Violated in her slumbers –
Mackie, how much did you charge?

Laughter among the whores. A man steps out from their midst and walks quickly away across the square.

LOW-DIVE JENNY: That was Mac the Knife!

ACT ONE

I

To combat the increasing callousness of mankind, J. Peachum, a man of business, has opened a shop where the poorest of the poor can acquire an exterior that will touch the hardest of hearts.

Jonathan Jeremiah Peacham's outfitting shop for beggars.

PEACHUM'S MORNING HYMN

You ramshackle Christian, awake!
Get on with your sinful employment
Show what a good crook you could make.
The Lord will cut short your enjoyment.

Betray your own brother, you rogue
And sell your old woman, you rat.
You think the Lord God's just a joke?
He'll give you His Judgement on that.

PEACHUM *to the audience:* Something new is needed. My business is too hard, for my business is arousing human sympathy. There are a few things that stir men's souls, just a few, but the trouble is that after repeated use they lose their effect. Because man has the abominable gift of being able to deaden his feelings at will, so to speak. Suppose, for instance, a man sees another man standing on the corner with a stump for an arm; the first time he may be shocked enough to give him tenpence, but the second time it will only be fivepence, and if he sees him a third time he'll hand him over to the police without batting an eyelash. It's the same with the spiritual approach. *A large sign saying 'It is more blessed to give than to receive' is lowered from the grid.* What good are the most beautiful, the most poignant sayings, painted on the most enticing little signs, when they get expended so quickly? The Bible has four or five sayings that stir the heart; once a man has expended them, there's nothing for it but starvation. Take this one, for instance – 'Give and it shall be given unto you' – how threadbare it is after hanging here a mere three weeks. Yes, you have to keep on offering something new. So it's back to the good old Bible again, but how long can it go on providing?

Knocking. Peachum opens. Enter a young man by the name of Filch.

FILCH: Messrs Peachum & Co.?

PEACHUM: Peachum.

FILCH: Are you the proprietor of The Beggar's Friend Ltd.? I've been sent to you. Fine slogans you've got there! Money in the bank, those are. Got a whole library full of them, I suppose? That's what I call really something. What chance has a bloke like me got to think up ideas like that; and how can business progress without education?

PEACHUM: What's your name?

FILCH: It's this way, Mr Peachum, I've been down on my luck since a boy. Mother drank, father gambled. Left to my own resources at an early age, without a mother's tender hand, I sank deeper and deeper into the quicksands of the big city. I've never known a father's care or the blessings of a happy home. So now you see me . . .

PEACHUM: So now I see you . . .

FILCH *confused:* . . . bereft of all support, a prey to my baser instincts.

PEACHUM: Like a derelict on the high seas and so on. Now tell me, derelict, which district have you been reciting that fairy story in?

FILCH: What do you mean, Mr Peachum?

PEACHUM: You deliver that speech in public, I take it?

FILCH: Well, it's this way, Mr Peachum, yesterday there was an unpleasant little incident in Highland Street. There I am, standing on the corner quiet and miserable, holding out my hat, no suspicion of anything nasty . . .

PEACHUM *leafs through a notebook:* Highland Street. Yes, yes, right. You're the bastard that Honey and Sam caught yesterday. You had the impudence to be molesting passers-by in District 10. We let you off with a thrashing because we had reason to believe you didn't know what's what. But if you show your face again it'll be the chop for you. Got it?

FILCH: Please, Mr Peachum, please. What can I do, Mr Peachum? The gentlemen beat me black and blue and then they gave me your business card. If I took off my coat, you'd think you were looking at a fish on a slab.

PEACHUM: My friend, if you're not flat as a kipper, then my men weren't doing their job properly. Along come these young whipper-snappers who think they've only got to hold out their paw to land a steak. What would you say if someone started fishing the best trout out of your pond?

FILCH: It's like this, Mr Peachum – I haven't got a pond.

PEACHUM: Licences are delivered to professionals only. *Points in a businesslike way to a map of the city.* London is divided into fourteen districts. Any man who intends to practise the craft of begging in any one of them needs a licence from Jonathan Jeremiah Peachum & Co. Why, anybody could come along – a prey to his baser instincts.

FILCH: Mr Peachum, only a few shillings stand between me and utter ruin. Something must be done. With two shillings in my pocket I . . .

PEACHUM: One pound.

FILCH: Mr Peachum!

Points imploringly at a sign saying 'Do not turn a deaf ear to misery!' Peachum points to the curtain over a showcase, on which is written: 'Give and it shall be given unto you!'

FILCH: Ten bob.

PEACHUM: Plus fifty per cent of your take, settle up once a week. With outfit seventy per cent.

FILCH: What does the outfit consist of?

PEACHUM: That's for the firm to decide.

FILCH: Which district could I start in?

PEACHUM: Baker Street. Numbers 2 to 104. That comes even cheaper. Only fifty per cent, including the outfit.

FILCH: Very well. *He pays.*

PEACHUM: Your name?

FILCH: Charles Filch.

PEACHUM: Right. *Shouts.* Mrs Peachum! *Mrs Peachum enters.* This is Filch. Number 314. Baker Street district. I'll do his entry myself. Trust you to pick this moment to apply, just before the Coronation, when for once in a lifetime there's a chance of making a little something. Outfit C. *He opens a linen curtain before a showcase in which there are five wax dummies.*

FILCH: What's that?

PEACHUM: Those are the five basic types of misery, those most likely to touch the human heart. The sight of such types puts a man into the unnatural state where he is willing to part with money. Outfit A: Victim of vehicular progress. The merry paraplegic, always cheerful – *He acts it out.* – always carefree, emphasised by arm-stump. Outfit B: Victim of the Higher Strategy. The Tiresome Trembler, molests passers-by, operates by inspiring nausea – *He acts it out.* – attenuated by medals. Outfit C: Victim of advanced Technology. The Pitiful Blind Man, the Cordon Bleu of Beggary.

He acts it out, staggering toward Filch. The moment he bumps into Filch, Filch cries out in horror. Peachum stops at once, looks at him with amazement and suddenly roars.

He's *sorry* for me! You'll never be a beggar as long as you live! You're only fit to be begged from! Very well, outfit D! Celia, you've been drinking again. And now you can't see straight. Number 136 has complained about his outfit. How often do I have to tell you that a gentleman doesn't put on filthy clothes? The only thing about it that could inspire pity was the stains and they should have been added by just ironing in candle wax. Use your head! Have I got to do everything myself? *To Filch:* Take off your clothes and put this on, but mind you, look after it!

FILCH: What about my things?

PEACHUM: Property of the firm. Outfit E: young man who has seen better days or, if you'd rather, never thought it would come to this.

FILCH: Oh, you use them again? Why can't *I* do the better days act?

PEACHUM: Because nobody can make his own suffering sound convincing, my boy. If you have a bellyache and say so, people will simply be disgusted. Anyway, you're not here to ask questions but to put these things on.

FILCH: Aren't they rather dirty? *After Peachum has given him a penetrating look.* Excuse me, sir, please excuse me.

MRS PEACHUM: Shake a leg, son, I'm not standing here holding your trousers till Christmas.

FILCH *suddenly emphatic:* But I'm not taking my shoes off! Absolutely not. I'd sooner pack the whole thing in. They're the only present my poor mother ever gave me, I may have sunk pretty low, but never . . .

MRS PEACHUM: Stop drivelling. We all know your feet are dirty.

FILCH: Where am I supposed to wash my feet? In midwinter?

Mrs Peachum leads him behind a screen, then she sits down on the left and starts ironing candle wax into a suit.

PEACHUM: Where's your daughter?

MRS PEACHUM: Polly? Upstairs.

PEACHUM: Has that man been here again? The one who's always coming round when I'm out?

MRS PEACHUM: Don't be so suspicious, Jonathan, there's no finer gentleman. The Captain takes a real interest in our Polly.

PEACHUM: I see.

MRS PEACHUM: And if I've got half an eye in my head, Polly thinks he's very nice too.

PEACHUM: Celia, the way you chuck your daughter around anyone would think I was a millionaire. Wanting to marry her off? The idea! Do you think this lousy business of ours would survive a week if those ragamuffins our customers had nothing better than *our* legs to look at? A husband! He'd have us in his clutches in three shakes! In his clutches! Do you think your daughter can hold her tongue in bed any better than you?

MRS PEACHUM: A fine opinion of your daughter you have.

PEACHUM: The worst. The very worst. A lump of sensuality, that's what she is.

MRS PEACHUM: If so, she didn't get it from you.

PEACHUM: Marriage! I expect my daughter to be to me as bread to the hungry. *He leafs in the Book.* It even says so in the Bible somewhere. Anyway marriage is disgusting. I'll teach her to get married.

MRS PEACHUM: Jonathan, you're just a barbarian.

PEACHUM: Barbarian! What's this gentleman's name?

MRS PEACHUM: They never call him anything but 'the Captain'.

PEACHUM: So you haven't even asked him his name? Interesting.

MRS PEACHUM: You don't suppose we'd ask for a birth certificate when such a distinguished gentleman invites Polly and me to the Cuttlefish Hotel for a little hop.

PEACHUM: Where?

MRS PEACHUM: To the Cuttlefish Hotel for a little hop.

PEACHUM: Captain? Cuttlefish Hotel? Hm, hm, hm . . .

MRS PEACHUM: A gentleman who has always handled me and my daughter with kid gloves.

PEACHUM: Kid gloves!

MRS PEACHUM: Honest, he always does wear gloves, white ones: white kid gloves.

PEACHUM: I see. White gloves and a cane with an ivory handle and spats and patent-leather shoes and a charismatic personality and a scar . . .

MRS PEACHUM: On his neck. Isn't there anyone you don't know?

Filch crawls out from behind the screen.

FILCH: Mr Peachum, couldn't you give me a few tips, I've always believed in having a system and not just shooting off my mouth any old how.

MRS PEACHUM: A system!

PEACHUM: He can be a half-wit. Come back this evening at six, we'll teach you the rudiments. Now piss off!

FILCH: Thank you very much indeed, Mr Peachum. Many thanks. *Goes out.*

PEACHUM: Fifty per cent! – And now I'll tell you who this

gentleman with the gloves is – Mac the Knife! *He runs up the stairs to Polly's bedroom.*

MRS PEACHUM: God in Heaven! Mac the Knife! Jesus! Gentle Jesus meek and mild – Polly! Where's Polly? *Peachum comes down slowly.*

PEACHUM: Polly? Polly's not come home. Her bed has not been slept in.

MRS PEACHUM: She'll have gone to supper with that wool merchant. That'll be it, Jonathan.

PEACHUM: Let's hope to God it is the wool merchant! *Mr and Mrs Peachum step before the curtain and sing. Song lighting: golden glow. The organ is lit up. Three lamps are lowered from above on a pole, and the signs say:*

THE 'NO THEY CAN'T' SONG

No, they can't
Bear to be at home all tucked up tight in bed.
It's fun they want
You can bet they've got some fancy notions brewing up
    instead.

So that's your Moon over Soho
That is your infernal 'd'you feel my heart beating?' line.
That's the old 'wherever you go I shall be with you,
    honey'
When you first fall in love and the moonbeams shine.

No, they can't
See what's good for them and set their mind on it.
It's fun they want
So they end up on their arses in the shit.

Then where's your Moon over Soho?
What's come of your infernal 'd'you feel my heart beat-
    ing?' bit?
Where's the old 'wherever you go I shall be with you,
    honey'?
When you're no more in love, and you're in the shit?

2

Deep in the heart of Soho the bandit Mac the Knife is celebrating his marriage to Polly Peachum, the beggar king's daughter.

Bare stable.

MATTHEW, *known as Matt of the Mint, holds out his revolver and searches the stable with a lantern:* Hey, hands up, anybody that's here!
Macheath enters and makes a tour of inspection along the footlights.
MACHEATH: Well, is there anybody?
MATTHEW: Not a soul. Just the place for our wedding.
POLLY *enters in wedding dress:* But it's a stable!
MAC: Sit on the feed-bin for the moment, Polly. *To the audience:* Today this stable will witness my marriage to Miss Polly Peachum, who has followed me for love in order to share my life with me.
MATTHEW: All over London they'll be saying this is the most daring job you've ever pulled, Mac, enticing Mr Peachum's only child from his home.
MAC: Who's Mr Peachum?
MATTHEW: He'll tell you he's the poorest man in London.
POLLY: But you can't be meaning to have our wedding here? Why, it is a common stable. You can't ask the vicar to a place like this. Besides, it isn't even ours. We really oughtn't to start our new life with a burglary, Mac. Why, this is the biggest day of our life.
MAC: Dear child, everything shall be done as you wish. We can't have you embarrassed in any way. The trimmings will be here in a moment.
MATTHEW: That'll be the furniture.
Large vans are heard driving up. Half a dozen men come in, carry-

*ing carpets, furniture, dishes, etc., with which they transform the
stable into an exaggeratedly luxurious room.*[1]*

MAC: Junk.

*The gentlemen put their presents down left, congratulate the bride
and report to the bridegroom.*[2]

JAKE *known as Crook-fingered Jake*: Congratulations! At 14
Ginger Street there were some people on the second floor.
We had to smoke them out.

BOB *known as Bob the Saw*: Congratulations! A copper got done
in the Strand.

MAC: Amateurs.

NED: We did all we could, but three people in the West End
were past saving. Congratulations!

MAC: Amateurs and bunglers.

JIMMY: An old gent got hurt a bit, but I don't think it's anything serious. Congratulations.

MAC: My orders were: avoid bloodshed. It makes me sick to
think of it. You'll never make business men! Cannibals,
perhaps, but not business men!

WALTER *known as Dreary Walt:* Congratulations. Only half an
hour ago, Madam, that harpsichord belonged to the
Duchess of Somerset.

POLLY: What is this furniture anyway?

MAC: How do you like the furniture, Polly?

POLLY *in tears:* Those poor people, all for a few sticks of
furniture.

MAC: And what furniture! Junk! You have a perfect right to
be angry. A rosewood harpsichord along with a renaissance
sofa. That's unforgivable. What about a table?

WALTER: A table?

They lay some planks over the bins.

POLLY: Oh, Mac, I'm so miserable! I only hope the vicar
doesn't come.

MATTHEW: Of course he'll come. We gave him exact
directions.

WALTER *introduces the table:* A table!

MAC *seeing Polly in tears:* My wife is very much upset. Where
are the rest of the chairs? A harpsichord and the happy

* These numbers refer to the 'Hints for actors' in the Notes p. 84 ff.

couple has to sit on the floor! Use your heads! For once I'm having a wedding, and how often does that happen? Shut up, Dreary! And how often does it happen that I leave you to do something on your own? And when I do you start by upsetting my wife.

NED: Dear Polly . . .

MAC *knocks his hat off his head*[3]: 'Dear Polly'! I'll bash your head through your kidneys with your 'dear Polly', you squirt. Have you ever heard the like? 'Dear Polly!' I suppose you've been to bed with her?

POLLY: Mac!

NED: I swear . . .

WALTER: Dear madam, if any items of furniture should be lacking, we'll be only too glad to go back and . . .

MAC: A rosewood harpsichord and no chairs. *Laughs*. Speaking as a bride, what do you say to that?

POLLY: It could be worse.

MAC: Two chairs and a sofa and the bridal couple has to sit on the floor.

POLLY: Something new, I'd say.

MAC *sharply:* Get the legs sawn off this harpsichord! Go on!

FOUR MEN *saw the legs off the harpsichord and sing:*

> Bill Lawgen and Mary Syer
> Were made man and wife a week ago.
> When it was over and they exchanged a kiss
> He was thinking 'Whose wedding dress was this?'
> While his name was one thing she'd rather like to know.
> Hooray!

WALTER: The finished article, madam: there's your bench.

MAC: May I now ask the gentlemen to take off those filthy rags and put on some decent clothes? This isn't just anybody's wedding, you know. Polly, may I ask you to look after the fodder?

POLLY: Is this our wedding feast? Was the whole lot stolen, Mac?

MAC: Of course. Of course.

POLLY: I wonder what you will do if there's a knock at the door and the sheriff steps in.

MAC: I'll show you what your husband will do in that situation.

MATTHEW: It couldn't happen today. The mounted police are all sure to be in Daventry. They'll be escorting the Queen back to town for Friday's Coronation.

POLLY: Two knives and fourteen forks! One knife per chair.

MAC: What incompetence! That's the work of apprentices, not experienced men! Haven't you any sense of style? Fancy not knowing the difference between Chippendale and Louis Quatorze.

The gang comes back. The gentlemen are now wearing fashionable evening dress, but unfortunately their movements are not in keeping with it.

WALTER: We only wanted to bring the most valuable stuff. Look at that wood! Really first class.

MATTHEW: Ssst! Ssst! Permit us, Captain . . .

MAC: Polly, come here a minute.

Mac and Polly assume the pose of a couple prepared to receive congratulations.

MATTHEW: Permit us, Captain, on the greatest day of your life, in the full bloom of your career, or rather the turning point, to offer you our heartiest and at the same time most sincere congratulations, etcetera. That posh talk don't half make me sick. So to cut a long story short – *Shakes Mac's hand.* – keep up the good work, old mate.

MAC: Thank you, that was kind of you, Matthew.

MATTHEW *shaking Polly's hand after embracing Mac with emotion:* It was spoken from the heart, all right! So as I was saying, keep it up, old china, I mean – *Grinning* – the good work of course.

Roars of laughter from the guests. Suddenly Mac with a deft movement sends Matthew to the floor.

MAC: Shut your trap. Keep that filth for Kitty, she's the kind of slut that appreciates it.

POLLY: Mac, don't be so vulgar.

MATTHEW: Here, I don't like that. Calling Kitty a slut . . . *Stands up with difficulty.*

MAC: Oh, so you don't like that?

MATTHEW: And besides, I never use filthy language with her. I respect Kitty too much. But maybe you wouldn't understand that, the way you are. You're a fine one to talk about filth. Do you think Lucy didn't tell me the things you've told her? Compared to that, I'm driven snow.

Mac looks at him.

JAKE: Cut it out, this is a wedding. *They pull him away.*

MAC: Fine wedding, isn't it, Polly? Having to see trash like this around you on the day of your marriage. You wouldn't have thought your husband's friends would let him down. Think about it.

POLLY: I think it's nice.

ROBERT: Blarney. Nobody's letting you down. What's a difference of opinion between friends? Kitty's as good as the next girl. But now bring out your wedding present, mate.

ALL: Yes, hand it over!

MATTHEW *offended:* Here.

POLLY: Oh, a wedding present. How kind of you, Mr Matt of the Mint. Look, Mac, what a lovely nightgown.

MATTHEW: Another bit of filth, eh, Captain?

MAC: Forget it. I didn't mean to hurt your feelings on this festive occasion.

WALTER: What do you say to this? Chippendale!

He unveils an enormous Chippendale grandfather clock.

MAC: Quatorze.

POLLY: It's wonderful. I'm so happy. Words fail me. You're so unbelievably kind. Oh, Mac, isn't it a shame we've no flat to put it in?

MAC: Hm, it's a start in the right direction. The great thing is to get started. Thank you kindly, Walter. Go on, clear the stuff away now. Food!

JAKE *while the others start setting the table:* Trust me to come empty-handed again. *Intensely to Polly:* Believe me, young lady, I find it most distressing.

POLLY: It doesn't matter in the least, Mr Crook-finger Jake.

JAKE: Here are the boys flinging presents right and left, and me standing here like a fool. What a situation to be in! It's always the way with me. Situations! It's enough to make your hair stand on end. The other day I meet Low-Dive Jenny; well, I say, you old cow . . .

Suddenly he sees Mac standing behind him and goes off without a word.

MAC *leads Polly to her place:* This is the best food you'll taste today, Polly. Gentlemen!

All sit down to the wedding feast.[4]

NED *indicating the china:* Beautiful dishes. Savoy Hotel.

JAKE: The plover's eggs are from Selfridge's. There was supposed to be a bucket of foie gras. But Jimmy ate it on the way, he was mad because it had a hole in it.

WALTER: We don't talk about holes in polite society.

JIMMY: Don't bolt your eggs like that, Ned, not on a day like this.

MAC: Couldn't somebody sing something? Something splendiferous?

MATTHEW *choking with laughter:* Something splendiferous? That's a first-class word. *He sits down in embarrassment under Mac's withering glance.*

MAC *knocks a bowl out of someone's hand:* I didn't mean us to start eating yet. Instead of seeing you people wade straight into the trough, I would have liked something from the heart. That's what other people do on this sort of occasion.

JAKE: What, for instance?

MAC: Am I supposed to think of everything myself? I'm not asking you to put on an opera. But you might have arranged for something else besides stuffing your bellies and making filthy jokes. Oh well, it's a day like this that you find out who your friends are.

POLLY: The salmon is marvellous, Mac.

NED: I bet you've never eaten anything like it. You get that every day at Mac the Knife's. You've landed in the honey pot all right. That's what I've always said: Mac is the right match for a girl with a feeling for higher things. As I was saying to Lucy only yesterday.

POLLY: Lucy? Mac, who is Lucy?

JAKE *embarrassed:* Lucy? Oh, nothing serious, you know.

Matthew has risen; standing behind Polly, he is waving his arms to shut Jake up.

POLLY *sees him:* Do you want something? Salt perhaps . . .? What were you saying, Mr Jake?

JAKE: Oh, nothing, nothing at all. The main thing I wanted to say really was nothing at all. I'm always putting my foot in it.

MAC: What have you got in your hand, Jake?

JAKE: A knife, Boss.

MAC: And what have you got on your plate?

JAKE: A trout, Boss.

MAC: I see. And with the knife you are eating the trout, are you not? It's incredible. Did you ever see the like of it, Polly? Eating his fish with a knife! Anybody who does that is just a plain swine, do you get me, Jake? Think about it. You'll have your hands full, Polly, trying to turn trash like this into a human being. Have you boys got the least idea what that is?

WALTER: A human being or a human pee-ing?

POLLY: Really, Mr Walter!

MAC: So you won't sing a song, something to brighten up the day? Has it got to be a miserable gloomy day like any other? And come to think of it, is anybody guarding the door? I suppose you want me to attend to that myself too? Do you want me on this day of days to guard the door so you lot can stuff your bellies at my expense?

WALTER *sullenly:* What do you mean at your expense?

JIMMY: Stow it, Walter boy. I'm on my way. Who's going to come here anyway? *Goes out.*

JAKE: A fine joke on a day like this if all the wedding guests were pulled in.

JIMMY *rushes in:* Hey, Captain. The cops!

WALTER: Tiger Brown!

MATTHEW: Nonsense, it's the Reverend Kimball.
    Kimball enters.

ALL *roar:* Good evening, Reverend Kimball!

KIMBALL: So I've found you after all. I find you in a lowly hut, a humble place but your own.

MAC: Property of the Duke of Devonshire.

POLLY: Good evening, Reverend. Oh, I'm so glad that on the happiest day of our life you . . .

MAC: And now I request a rousing song for the Reverend Kimball.

MATTHEW: How about Bill Lawgen and Mary Syer?

JAKE: Good. Bill Lawgen might be just the thing.

KIMBALL: Be nice if you'd do a little number, boys.

MATTHEW: Let's have it, gentlemen.

Three men rise and sing hesitantly, weakly and uncertainly:

WEDDING SONG FOR THE LESS WELL-OFF

Bill Lawgen and Mary Syer
Were made man and wife a week ago
(Three cheers for the happy couple: hip, hip, hooray!)
When it was over and they exchanged a kiss
He was thinking 'Whose wedding dress was this?'
While his name was one thing she'd rather like to know.
Hooray!

Do you know what your wife's up to? No!
Do you like her sleeping round like that? No!
Three cheers for the happy couple: Hip, hip, hooray!
Billy Lawgen told me recently
Just one part of her will do for me.
The swine.
Hooray!

MAC: Is that all? Penurious!

MATTHEW *chokes again:* Penurious is the word, gentlemen.

MAC: Shut your trap!

MATTHEW: Oh, I only meant no gusto, no fire, and so on.

POLLY: Gentlemen, if none of you wishes to perform, I myself will sing a little song; it's an imitation of a girl I saw once in some twopenny-halfpenny dive in Soho. She was washing the glasses, and everybody was laughing at her, and then she turned to the guests and said things like the things I'm going to sing to you. Right. This is a little bar, I want you to think of it as filthy. She stood behind it morning and night. This is the bucket and this is the rag she washed the glasses with. Where you are sitting, the customers were sitting laughing at her. You can laugh too, to make it exactly the same; but if you don't want to, you don't have to. *She starts pretending to wash glasses, muttering to herself.* Now, for instance, one of them – it might be you – *Pointing at Walter* – says: Well, when's your ship coming in, Jenny?

WALTER: Well, when's your ship coming in, Jenny?

POLLY: And another says – you, for instance: Still washing up glasses, Jenny the pirate's bride?

MATTHEW: Still washing up glasses, Jenny the pirate's bride?

POLLY: Good. And now I'll begin.

Song lighting: golden glow. The organ is lit up. Three lamps are lowered from above on a pole, and the signs say:

PIRATE JENNY

Now you gents all see I've the glasses to wash.
When a bed's to be made I make it.
You may tip me with a penny, and I'll thank you very
    well
And you see me dressed in tatters, and this tatty old hotel
And you never ask how long I'll take it.
But one of these evenings there will be screams from the
    harbour
And they'll ask: what can all that screaming be?
And they'll see me smiling as I do the glasses
And they'll say: how she can smile beats me.
        And a ship with eight sails and
        All its fifty guns loaded
        Has tied up at the quay.

They say: get on, dry your glasses, my girl
And they tip me and don't give a damn.
And their penny is accepted, and their bed will be made
(Although nobody is going to sleep there, I'm afraid)
And they still have no idea who I am.
But one of these evenings there will be explosions from
    the harbour,
And they'll ask: what kind of a bang was that?

And they'll see me as I stand beside the window
And they'll say: what has she got to smile at?
    And that ship with eight sails and
    All its fifty guns loaded
    Will lay siege to the town.

Then you gents, you aren't going to find it a joke
For the walls will be knocked down flat
And in no time the town will be rased to the ground.
Just one tatty old hotel will be left standing safe and
    sound
And they'll ask: did someone special live in that?
Then there'll be a lot of people milling round the hotel
And they'll ask: what made them let that place alone?
And they'll see me as I leave the door next morning
And they'll say: don't tell us she's the one.
    And that ship with eight sails and
    All its fifty guns loaded
    Will run up its flag.

And a hundred men will land in the bright midday sun
Each stepping where the shadows fall.
They'll look inside each doorway and grab anyone they
    see
And put him in irons and then bring him to me
And they'll ask: which of these should we kill?
In that noonday heat there'll be a hush round the harbour
As they ask which has got to die.
And you'll hear me as I softly answer: the lot!
And as the first head rolls I'll say: hoppla!
    And that ship with eight sails and
    All its fifty guns loaded
    Will vanish with me.

MATTHEW: Very nice. Cute, eh? The way the missus puts it
across!
MAC: What do you mean nice? It's not nice, you idiot! It's
art, it's not nice. You did that marvellously, Polly. But it's
wasted on trash like this, if you'll excuse me, your Rever-

ence. *In an undertone to Polly:* Anyway, I don't like you play-acting; let's not have any more of it.

Laughter at the table. The gang is making fun of the parson.

What you got in your hand, your Reverence?

JAKE: Two knives, Captain.

MAC: What you got on your plate, your Reverence?

KIMBALL: Salmon, I think.

MAC: And with that knife you are eating the salmon, are you not?

JAKE: Did you ever see the like of it, eating fish with a knife? Anybody who does that is just a plain . . .

MAC: Swine. Do you understand me, Jake? Think about it.

JIMMY *rushing in:* Hey, Captain, coppers. The sheriff in person.

WALTER: Brown. Tiger Brown!

MAC: Yes, Tiger Brown, exactly. It's Tiger Brown himself, the Chief Sheriff of London, pillar of the Old Bailey, who will now enter Captain Macheath's humble abode. Think about it.

The bandits creep away.

JAKE: It'll be the drop for us!

Brown enters.

MAC: Hullo, Jackie.

BROWN: Hullo, Mac! I haven't much time, got to be leaving in a minute. Does it have to be somebody else's stable? Why, this is breaking and entering again!

MAC: But Jackie, it's such a good address. I'm glad you could come to old Mac's wedding. Let me introduce my wife, née Peachum. Polly, this is Tiger Brown, what do you say, old man? *Slaps him on the back.* And these are my friends, Jackie, I imagine you've seen them all before.

BROWN *pained:* I'm here unofficially, Mac.

MAC: So are they. *He calls them. They come in with their hands up.* Hey, Jake.

BROWN: That's Crook-fingered Jake. He's a dirty dog.

MAC: Hey, Jimmy; hey, Bob; hey, Walter!

BROWN: Well, just for today I'll turn a blind eye.

MAC: Hey, Ned; hey, Matthew.

BROWN: Be seated, gentlemen, be seated.

ALL: Thank you, sir.

BROWN: I'm delighted to meet my old friend Mac's charming wife.

POLLY: Don't mention it, sir.

MAC: Sit down, you old bugger, and pitch into the whisky! – Polly and gentlemen! You have today in your midst a man whom the king's inscrutable wisdom has placed high above his fellow men and who has none the less remained my friend throughout the storms and perils, and so on. You know who I mean, and you too know who I mean, Brown. Ah, Jackie, do you remember how we served in India together, soldiers both of us? Ah, Jackie, let's sing the Cannon Song right now.

They sit down on the table.

Song lighting: golden glow. The organ is lit up. Three lamps are lowered from above on a pole, and the signs say:

THE CANNON SONG

John was all present and Jim was all there
And Georgie was up for promotion.
Not that the army gave a bugger who they were
When confronting some heathen commotion.
    The troops live under
    The cannon's thunder
    From the Cape to Cooch Behar.
    Moving from place to place
    When they come face to face
    With a different breed of fellow
    Whose skin is black or yellow
    They quick as winking chop him into beefsteak
       tartare.

Johnny found his whisky too warm
And Jim found the weather too balmy
But Georgie took them both by the arm
And said: never let down the army.
    The troops live under
    The cannon's thunder

From the Cape to Cooch Behar.
Moving from place to place
When they come face to face
With a different breed of fellow
Whose skin is black or yellow
They quick as winking chop him into beefsteak
tartare.

John is a write-off and Jimmy is dead
And they shot poor old Georgie for looting
But young men's blood goes on being red
And the army goes on recruiting.
The troops live under
The cannon's thunder
From the Cape to Cooch Behar.
Moving from place to place
When they come face to face
With a different breed of fellow
Whose skin is black or yellow
They quick as winking chop him into beefsteak
tartare.

MAC: Though life with its raging torrent has carried us boyhood friends far apart, although our professional interests
are very different, some people would go so far as to say
diametrically opposed, our friendship has come through
unimpaired. Think about it. Castor and Pollux, Hector and
Andromache, etcetera. Seldom have I, the humble bandit,
well, you know what I mean, made even the smallest haul
without giving him, my friend, a share, a substantial share,
Brown, as a gift and token of my unswerving loyalty, and
seldom has he, take that knife out of your mouth, Jake, the
all-powerful police chief, staged a raid without sending me,
his boyhood friend, a little tip-off. Well, and so on and so
forth, it's all a matter of give and take. Think about it. *He
takes Brown by the arm.* Well, Jackie, old man, I'm glad
you've come, I call that real friendship. *Pause, because Brown
has been looking sadly at a carpet.* Genuine Shiraz.
BROWN: From the Oriental Carpet Company.

MAC: Yes, we never go anywhere else. Do you know, Jackie, I had to have you here today, I hope it's not awkward for you in your position?

BROWN: You know, Mac, that I can't refuse you anything. I must be going, I've really got so much on my plate; if the slightest thing should go wrong at the Queen's Coronation . . .

MAC: See here, Jackie, my father-in-law is a revolting old bastard. If he tries to make trouble for me, is there anything on record against me at Scotland Yard?

BROWN: There's nothing whatsoever on record against you at Scotland Yard.

MAC: I knew it.

BROWN: I've taken care of that. Good night.

MAC: Aren't you fellows going to stand up?

BROWN *to Polly:* Best of luck. *Goes out accompanied by Mac.*

JAKE *who along with Matthew and Walter has meanwhile been conferring with Polly:* I must admit I couldn't repress a certain alarm a while ago when I heard Tiger Brown was coming.

MATTHEW: You see, dear lady, we have contacts in the highest places.

WALTER: Yes, Mac always has some iron in the fire that the rest of us don't even suspect. But we have our own little iron in the fire. Gentlemen, it's half-past nine.

MATTHEW: And now comes the *pièce de résistance.*
All go upstage behind the carpet that conceals something. Mac enters.

MAC: I say, what's going on?

MATTHEW: Hey, Captain, another little surprise.
Behind the curtain they sing the Bill Lawgen song softly and with much feeling. But at 'his name was one thing she'd rather like to know' Matthew pulls down the carpet and all go on with the song, bellowing and pounding on the bed that has been disclosed.

MAC: Thank you, friends, thank you.

WALTER: And now we shall quietly take our leave.
The gang go out.

MAC: And now the time has come for softer sentiments. Without them man is a mere beast of burden. Sit down, Polly.
Music.

MAC: Look at the moon over Soho.

POLLY: I see it, dearest. Feel my heart beating, my beloved.

MAC: I feel it, beloved.

POLLY: Where'er you go I shall be with you.

MAC: And where you stay, there too shall I be.

BOTH:

> And though we've no paper to say we're wed
> And no altar covered with flowers
> And nobody knows for whom your dress was made
> And even the ring is not ours –
> The platter off which you've been eating your bread
> Give it one brief look; fling it far.
> For love will endure or not endure
> Regardless of where we are.

3

To Peachum, conscious of the hardness of the world, the loss of his daughter means utter ruin.

Peachum's Outfitting Emporium for Beggars.

To the right Peachum and Mrs Peachum. In the doorway stands Polly in her coat and hat, holding her travelling bag.

MRS PEACHUM: Married? First you rig her fore and aft in dresses and hats and gloves and parasols, and when she's cost as much as a sailing ship, she throws herself in the garbage like a rotten pickle. Are you really married? *Song lighting: golden glow. The organ is lit up. Three lamps are lowered from above on a pole and the signs say:*

IN A LITTLE SONG POLLY GIVES HER PARENTS TO
UNDERSTAND THAT SHE HAS MARRIED THE
BANDIT MACHEATH:

I once used to think, in my innocent youth
(And I once was as innocent as you)
That someone someday might come my way
And then how should I know what's best to do?
And if he'd got money
And seemed a nice chap
And his workday shirts were white as snow
And if he knew how to treat a girl with due respect
I'd have to tell him: No.
    That's where you must keep your head screwed on
    And insist on going slow.
    Sure, the moon will shine throughout the night
    Sure, the boat is on the river, tied up tight.
    That's as far as things can go.
    Oh, you can't lie back, you must stay cold at heart
    Oh, you must not let your feelings show.
    Oh, whenever you feel it might start
    Ah, then your only answer's: No.

The first one that came was a man of Kent
And all that a man ought to be.
The second one owned three ships down at Wapping
And the third was crazy about me.
And as they'd got money
And all seemed nice chaps
And their workday shirts were white as snow
And as they knew how to treat a girl with due respect
Each time I told them: No.
    That's where I still kept my head screwed on
    And I chose to take it slow.
    Sure, the moon could shine throughout the night
    Sure, the boat was on the river, tied up tight
    That's as far as things could go.
    Oh, you can't lie back, you must stay cold at heart

Oh, you must not let your feelings show.
Oh, whenever you feel it might start
Ah, then your only answer's: No.

But then one day, and that day was blue
Came someone who didn't ask at all
And he went and hung his hat on the nail in my little
     attic
And what happened I can't quite recall.
And as he'd got no money
And was not a nice chap
And his Sunday shirts, even, were not like snow
And as he'd no idea of treating a girl with due respect
I could not tell him: No.
          That's the time my head was not screwed on
          And to hell with going slow.
          Oh, the moon was shining clear and bright
          Oh, the boat kept drifting downstream all that night
          That was how it simply had to go.
          Yes, you must lie back, you can't stay cold at heart
          In the end you have to let your feelings show.
          Oh, the moment you know it must start
          Ah, then's no time for saying: No.

PEACHUM: So she's associating with criminals. That's lovely.
     That's delightful.
MRS PEACHUM: If you're immoral enough to get married,
     did it have to be a horse-thief and a highwayman? That'll
     cost you dear one of these days! I ought to have seen it
     coming. Even as a child she had a swollen head like the
     Queen of England.
PEACHUM: So she's really got married!
MRS PEACHUM: Yes, yesterday, at five in the afternoon.
PEACHUM: To a notorious criminal. Come to think of it, it
     shows that the fellow is really audacious. If I give away my
     daughter, the sole prop of my old age, why, my house will
     cave in and my last dog will run off. I'd think twice about
     giving away the dirt under my fingernails, it would mean
     risking starvation. If the three of us can get through the

winter on one log of wood, maybe we'll live to see the new year. Maybe.

MRS PEACHUM: What got into you? This is our reward for all we've done, Jonathan. I'm going mad. My head is swimming. I'm going to faint. Oh! *She faints.* A glass of Cordial Médoc.

PEACHUM: You see what you've done to your mother. Quick! Associating with criminals, that's lovely, that's delightful! Interesting how the poor woman takes it to heart. *Polly brings in a bottle of Cordial Médoc.* That's the only consolation your poor mother has left.

POLLY: Go ahead, give her two glasses. *My* mother can take twice as much when she's not quite herself. That will put her back on her feet. *During the whole scene she looks very happy.*

MRS PEACHUM *wakes up:* Oh, there she goes again, pretending to be so loving and sympathetic!

Five men enter.[5]

BEGGAR: I'm making a complaint, see, this thing is a mess, it's not a proper stump, it's a botch-up, and I'm not wasting my money on it.

PEACHUM: What do you expect? It's as good a stump as any other; it's just that you don't keep it clean.

BEGGAR: Then why don't I take as much money as the others? Naw, you can't do that to me. *Throws down the stump.* If I wanted crap like this, I could cut off my real leg.

PEACHUM: What do you fellows want anyway? Is it my fault if people have hearts of flint? I can't make you five stumps. In five minutes I can turn any man into such a pitiful wreck it would make a dog weep to see him. Is it my fault if people don't weep? Here's another stump for you if one's not enough. But look after your equipment!

BEGGAR: This one will do.

PEACHUM *tries a false limb on another:* Leather is no good, Celia; rubber is more repulsive. *To the third:* That swelling is going down and it's your last. Now we'll have to start all over again. *Examining the fourth:* Of course natural scabies is never as good as the artificial kind. *To the fifth:* You're a sight! You've been eating again. I'll have to make an example of you.

BEGGAR: Mr Peachum, I really haven't eaten anything much. I'm just abnormally fat, I can't help it.

PEACHUM: Nor can I. You're fired. *Again to the second beggar:* My dear man, there's an obvious difference between 'tugging at people's heart strings' and 'getting on people's nerves'. Yes, artists, that's what I need. Only an artist can tug at anybody's heart strings nowadays. If you fellows performed properly, your audience would be forced to applaud. You just haven't any ideas! Obviously I can't extend your engagement.

The beggars go out.

POLLY: Look. Is he particularly handsome? No. But he makes a living. He can support me. He is not only a first-class burglar but a far-sighted and experienced stick-up man as well. I've been into it, I can tell you the exact amount of his savings to date. A few successful ventures and we shall be able to retire to a little house in the country just like that Mr Shakespeare father admires so much.

PEACHUM: It's quite simple. You're married. What does a girl do when she's married? Use your head. Well, she gets divorced, see. Is that so hard to figure out?

POLLY: I don't know what you're talking about.

MRS PEACHUM: Divorce.

POLLY: But I love him. How can I think of divorce?

MRS PEACHUM: Really, have you no shame?

POLLY: Mother, if you've ever been in love . . .

MRS PEACHUM: In love! Those damn books you've been reading have turned your head. Why, Polly, everybody's doing it.

POLLY: Then I'm an exception.

MRS PEACHUM: Then I'm going to tan your behind, you exception.

POLLY: Oh yes, all mothers do that, but it doesn't help because love goes deeper than a tanned behind.

MRS PEACHUM: Don't strain my patience.

POLLY: I won't let my love be taken away from me.

MRS PEACHUM: One more word out of you and you'll get a clip on the ear.

POLLY: But love is the finest thing in the world.

MRS PEACHUM: Anyway, he's got several women, the black-guard. When he's hanged, like as not half a dozen widows will turn up, each of them like as not with a brat in her arms. Oh, Jonathan!

PEACHUM: Hanged, what made you think of that, that's a good idea. Run along, Polly. *Polly goes out.* Quite right. That'll earn us forty pounds.

MRS PEACHUM: I see. Report him to the sheriff.

PEACHUM: Naturally. And besides, that way we get him hanged free of charge . . . Two birds with one stone. Only we've got to find out where he's holed up.

MRS PEACHUM: I can tell you that, my dear, he's holed up with his tarts.

PEACHUM: But they won't turn him in.

MRS PEACHUM: Just let me attend to that. Money rules the world. I'll go to Turnbridge right away and talk to the girls. Give us a couple of hours, and after that if he meets a single one of them he's done for.

POLLY *has been listening behind the door:* Dear Mama, you can spare yourself the trip. Mac will go to the Old Bailey of his own accord sooner than meet any of those ladies. And even if he did go to the Old Bailey, the sheriff would serve him a cocktail; they'd smoke their cigars and have a little chat about a certain shop in this street where a little more goes on than meets the eye. Because, Papa dear, the sheriff was very cheerful at my wedding.

PEACHUM: What's this sheriff called?

POLLY: He's called Brown. But you probably know him as Tiger Brown. Because everyone who has reason to fear him calls him Tiger Brown. But my husband, you see, calls him Jackie. Because to him he's just dear old Jackie. They're boyhood friends.

PEACHUM: Oh, so they're friends, are they? The sheriff and Public Enemy No. 1, ha, they must be the only friends in this city.

POLLY *poetically:* Every time they drank a cocktail together, they stroked each other's cheeks and said: 'If you'll have the same again, I'll have the same again.' And every time one of them left the room, the other's eyes grew moist and he said: 'Where'er you go I shall be with you.' There's nothing on record against Mac at Scotland Yard.

PEACHUM: I see. Between Tuesday evening and Thursday morning Mr Macheath, a gentleman who has assuredly been married many times, lured my daughter from her home on pretext of marriage. Before the week is out, he will be taken to the gallows on that account, and deservedly so. 'Mr Macheath, you once had white kid gloves, a cane with an ivory handle, and a scar on your neck, and frequented the Cuttlefish Hotel. All that is left is your scar, undoubtedly the least valuable of your distinguishing marks, and today you frequent nothing but prison cells, and within the foreseeable future no place at all . . .'

MRS PEACHUM: Oh, Jonathan, you'll never bring it off. Why, he's Mac the Knife, whom they call the biggest criminal in London. He takes what he pleases.

PEACHUM: Who's Mac the Knife? Get ready, we're going to see the Sheriff of London. And you're going to Turnbridge.

MRS PEACHUM: To see his whores.

PEACHUM: For the villainy of the world is great, and a man needs to run his legs off to keep them from being stolen from under him.

POLLY: I, Papa, shall be delighted to shake hands with Mr Brown again.

All three step forward and sing the first finale. Song lighting. On the signs is written:

FIRST THREE-PENNY FINALE
CONCERNING THE INSECURITY OF THE HUMAN CONDITION

POLLY:
Am I reaching for the sky?
All I'm asking from this place is
To enjoy a man's embraces.
Is that aiming much too high?
　　　　PEACHUM *with a Bible in his hand:*
Man has a right, in this our brief existence
To call some fleeting happiness his own

Partake of worldly pleasures and subsistence
And have bread on his table rather than a stone.
Such are the basic rights of man's existence.
But do we know of anything suggesting
That when a thing's a right one gets it? No!
To get one's rights would be most interesting
But our condition's such it can't be so.

MRS PEACHUM:

How I want what's best for you
How I'd teach you airs and graces
Show you things and take you places
As a mother likes to do.

PEACHUM:

Let's practise goodness: who would disagree?
Let's give our wealth away: is that not right?
Once all are good His Kingdom is at hand
Where blissfully we'll bask in His pure light.
Let's practise goodness: who would disagree?
But sadly on this planet while we're waiting
The means are meagre and the morals low.
To get one's record straight would be elating
But our condition's such it can't be so.

POLLY AND MRS PEACHUM:

So that is all there is to it.
The world is poor, and man's a shit.

PEACHUM:

Of course that's all there is to it.
The world is poor, and man's a shit.
Who wouldn't like an earthly paradise?
Yet our condition's such it can't arise.
Out of the question in our case.
Let's say your brother's close to you
But if there's not enough for two
He'll kick you smartly in the face.
You think that loyalty's no disgrace?
But say your wife is close to you
And finds she's barely making do
She'll kick you smartly in the face.
And gratitude: that's no disgrace

But say your son is close to you
And finds your pension's not come through
He'll kick you smartly in the face.
And so will all the human race.

POLLY AND MRS PEACHUM:

That's what you're all ignoring
That's what's so bloody boring.
The world is poor, and man's a shit
And that is all there is to it.

PEACHUM:

Of course that's all there is to it
The world is poor, and man's a shit.
We should aim high instead of low
But our condition's such this can't be so.

ALL THREE:

Which means He has us in a trap:
The whole damn thing's a load of crap.

PEACHUM:

The world is poor, and man's a shit
And that is all there is to it.

ALL THREE:

That's what you're all ignoring
That's what's so bloody boring.
That's why He's got us in a trap
And why it's all a load of crap.

4

Thursday afternoon: Mac the Knife takes leave of
his wife and flees from his father-in-law to the
heaths of Highgate.

The stable.

POLLY *enters:* Mac! Mac, don't be frightened.

MAC *lying on the bed:* Well, what's up? Polly, you look a
wreck.

POLLY: I've been to see Brown, my father went too, they
decided to pull you in; my father made some terrible threats
and Brown stood up for you, but then he weakened, and
now he thinks too that you'd better stir yourself and make
yourself scarce for a while, Mac. You must pack right
away.

MAC: Pack? Nonsense. Come here, Polly. You and I have got
better things to do than pack.

POLLY: No, we mustn't now. I'm so frightened. All they
talked about was hanging.

MAC: I don't like it when you're moody, Polly. There's
nothing on record against me at Scotland Yard.

POLLY: Perhaps there wasn't yesterday, but suddenly today
there's an awful lot. You – I've brought the charges with
me, I don't even know if I can get them straight, the list
goes on so. You've killed two shopkeepers, more than
thirty burglaries, twenty-three hold-ups, and God knows
how many acts of arson, attempted murder, forgery and
perjury, all within eighteen months. You're a dreadful man.
And in Winchester you seduced two sisters under the age of
consent.

MAC: They told me they were over twenty. What did Brown say?

He stands up slowly and goes whistling to the right along the foot-lights.

POLLY: He caught up with me in the corridor and said there was nothing he could do for you now. Oh, Mac! *She throws herself on his neck.*

MAC: All right, if I've got to go away, you'll have to run the business.

POLLY: Don't talk about business now, Mac, I can't bear it. Kiss your poor Polly again and swear that you'll never never be . . .

Mac interrupts her brusquely and leads her to the table where he pushes her down in a chair.

MAC: Here are the ledgers. Listen carefully. This is a list of the personnel. *Reads.* Hm, first of all, Crook-finger Jake, a year and a half in the business. Let's see what he's brought in. One, two, three, four, five gold watches, not much, but clean work. Don't sit on my lap, I'm not in the mood right now. Here's Dreary Walter, an unreliable sod. Sells stuff on the side. Give him three weeks' grace, then get rid of him. Just turn him in to Brown.

POLLY *sobbing:* Just turn him in to Brown.

MAC: Jimmy II, cheeky bastard; good worker but cheeky. Swipes bed sheets right out from under ladies of the best society. Give him a rise.

POLLY: I'll give him a rise.

MAC: Robert the Saw: small potatoes, not a glimmer of genius. Won't end on the gallows, but he won't leave any estate either.

POLLY: Won't leave any estate either.

MAC: In all other respects you will carry on exactly the same as before. Get up at seven, wash, have your weekly bath and so on.

POLLY: You're perfectly right, I'll have to grit my teeth and look after the business. What's yours is mine now, isn't it, Mackie? What about your chambers, Mac? Should I let them go? I don't like having to pay the rent.

MAC: No, I still need them.

POLLY: What for, it's just a waste of our money!

MAC: Oh, so you think I won't be coming back at all, do you?

POLLY: What do you mean? You can rent other rooms.[6] Mac
... Mac, I can't go on. I keep looking at your lips and then
I don't hear what you say. Will you be faithful to me, Mac?

MAC: Of course I'll be faithful, I'll do as I'm done by. Do you
think I don't love you? It's only that I see farther ahead
than you.

POLLY: I'm so grateful to you, Mac. Worrying about me
when they're after you like bloodhounds ...

*Hearing the word 'bloodhounds' he goes stiff, stands up, goes to the
right, throws off his coat and washes his hands.*

MAC *hastily:* You will go on sending the profits to Jack
Poole's banking house in Manchester. Between ourselves
it's only a matter of weeks before I go over to banking
altogether. It's safer and it's more profitable. In two weeks
at the most the money will have to be taken out of this
business, then off you go to Brown and give the list to the
police. Within four weeks all that human scum will be
safely in the cells at the Old Bailey.

POLLY: Why, Mac! How can you look them in the eye when
you've written them off and they're as good as hanged?
How can you shake hands with them?

MAC: With who? Robert the Saw, Matt of the Mint, Crook-
fingered Jake? Those gaol-birds?

Enter the gang.

MAC: Gentlemen, it's a pleasure to see you.

POLLY: Good evening, gentlemen.

MATTHEW: I've got hold of the Coronation programme,
Captain. It looks to me like we're going to be very busy in
the next few days. The Archbishop of Canterbury is arriv-
ing in half an hour.

MAC: When?

MATTHEW: Five thirty. We'd better be shoving off, Captain.

MAC: Yes, you'd better be shoving off.

ROBERT: What do you mean: you?

MAC: For my part, I'm afraid I'm obliged to take a little trip.

ROBERT: Good God, are they out to nab you?

MATTHEW: It would be just now, with the Coronation coming up! A Coronation without you is like porridge without a spoon.

MAC: Shut your trap! In view of that, I am temporarily handing over the management of the business to my wife.

He pushes her forward and goes to the rear where he observes her.

POLLY: Well, boys, I think the Captain can go away with an easy mind. We'll swing this job, you bet. What do you say, boys?

MATTHEW: It's no business of mine. But at a time like this I'm not so sure that a woman . . . I'm not saying anything against you, Ma'am.

MAC *from upstage:* What do you say to that, Polly?

POLLY: You shit, that's a fine way to start in. *Screaming.* Of course you're not saying anything against me! If you were, these gentlemen would have ripped your pants off long ago and tanned your arse for you. Wouldn't you, gentlemen? *Brief pause, then all clap like mad.*

JAKE: Yes, there's something in that, you can take her word for it.

WALTER: Hurrah, the missus knows how to lay it on! Hurrah for Polly!

ALL: Hurrah for Polly!

MAC: The rotten part of it is that I won't be here for the Coronation. There's a gilt-edged deal for you. In the day time nobody's home and at night the toffs are all drunk. That reminds me, you drink too much, Matthew. Last week you suggested it was you set the Greenwich Children's Hospital on fire. If such a thing occurs again, you're out. Who set the Children's Hospital on fire?

MATTHEW: I did.

MAC *to the others:* Who set it on fire?

THE OTHERS: You, Mr Macheath.

MAC: So who did it?

MATTHEW *sulkily:* You, Mr Macheath. At this rate our sort will never rise in the world.

MAC *with a gesture of stringing up:* You'll rise all right if you think you can compete with me. Who ever heard of one of those professors at Oxford College letting some assistant put his name to his mistakes? He puts his own.

ROBERT: Ma'am, while your husband is away, you're the boss. We settle up every Thursday, ma'am.

POLLY: Every Thursday, boys.

The gang goes out.

MAC: And now farewell, my heart. Look after your complexion, and don't forget to make up every day, exactly as if I were here. That's very important, Polly.

POLLY: And you, Mac, promise me you won't look at another woman and that you'll leave town right away. Believe me, it's not jealousy that makes your little Polly say that; no, it's very important, Mac.

MAC: Oh, Polly, why should I go round drinking up the empties? I love only you. As soon as the twilight is deep enough I'll take my black stallion from somebody's stable and before you can see the moon from your window, I'll be the other side of Highgate Heath.

POLLY: Oh, Mac, don't tear the heart out of my body. Stay with me and let us be happy.

MAC: But I must tear my own heart out of my body, for I must go away and no one knows when I shall return.

POLLY: It's been such a short time, Mac.

MAC: Does it have to be the end?

POLLY: Oh, last night I had a dream. I was looking out the window and I heard laughter in the street, and when I looked out I saw our moon and the moon was all thin like a worn-down penny. Don't forget me, Mac, in strange cities.

MAC: Of course I won't forget you, Polly. Kiss me, Polly.

POLLY: Goodbye, Mac.

MAC: Goodbye, Polly. *On his way out:*
    For love will endure or not endure
    Regardless of where we are.

POLLY *alone:* He never will come back. *She sings:*
    Nice while it lasted, and now it is over
    Tear out your heart, and goodbye to your lover!
    What's the use of grieving, when the mother that bore
       you
    (Mary, pity women!) knew it all before you?
    The bells start ringing.

POLLY:

>Into this London the Queen now makes her way.
>Where shall we be on Coronation Day?

Interlude

Mrs Peachum and Low-Dive Jenny step out before the curtain.

MRS PEACHUM: So if you see Mac the Knife in the next few days, run to the nearest constable and turn him in; it'll earn you ten shillings.

JENNY: Shall we see him, though, if the constables are after him? If the hunt is on, he won't go spending his time with us.

MRS PEACHUM: Take it from me, Jenny, even with all London at his heels, Macheath is not the man to give up his habits. *She sings:*

THE BALLAD OF SEXUAL OBSESSION

>There goes a man who's won his spurs in battle
>The butcher, he. And all the others, cattle.
>The cocky sod! No decent place lets him in.
>Who does him down, that's done the lot? The women.
>Want it or not, he can't ignore that call.
>Sexual obsession has him in its thrall.
>>He doesn't read the Bible. He sniggers at the law
>>Sets out to be an utter egoist
>>And knows a woman's skirts are what he must resist
>>So when a woman calls he locks his door.
>>So far, so good, but what's the future brewing?
>>As soon as night falls he'll be up and doing.

>Thus many a man watched men die in confusion:
>A mighty genius, stuck on prostitution!
>The watchers claimed their urges were exhausted
>But when they died who paid the funeral? Whores did.
>Want it or not, they can't ignore that call.
>Sexual obsession has them in its thrall.

Some fall back on the Bible. Some stick to the law
Some turn to Christ and some turn anarchist.
At lunch you pick the best wine on the list
Then meditate till half-past four.
At tea: what high ideals you are pursuing!
Then soon as night falls you'll be up and doing.

5

Before the Coronation bells had died away, Mac
the Knife was sitting with the whores of Turnbridge! The whores betray him. It is Thursday
evening.

Whorehouse in Turnbridge.

*An afternoon like any other; the whores, mostly in their shifts, are
ironing clothes, playing draughts, or washing: a bourgeois idyll.[7]
Crook-fingered Jake is reading the newspaper. No one pays any
attention to him. He is rather in the way.*

JAKE: He won't come today.
WHORE: No?
JAKE: I don't think he'll ever come again.
WHORE: That would be a pity.
JAKE: Think so? If I know him, he's out of town by now.
   This time he's really cleared out.
   *Enter Macheath, hangs his hat on a nail, sits down on the sofa
   behind the table.*
MAC: My coffee!
VIXEN *repeats admiringly:* 'My coffee!'
JAKE *horrified:* Why aren't you in Highgate?
MAC: It's my Thursday. Do you think I can let such trifles
   interfere with my habits? *Throws the warrant on the floor.*
   Anyhow, it's raining.

JENNY *reads the warrant:* In the name of the King, Captain Macheath is charged with three . . .

JAKE *takes it away from her:* Am I in it too?

MAC: Naturally, the whole team.

JENNY *to the other whore:* Look, that's the warrant. *Pause.* Mac, let's see your hand. *He gives her his hand.*

DOLLY: That's right, Jenny, read his palm, you do it so well. *Holds up an oil lamp.*

MAC: Coming into money?

JENNY: No, not coming into money.

BETTY: What's that look for, Jenny? It gives me the shivers.

MAC: A long journey?

JENNY: No, no long journey.

VIXEN: What *do* you see?

MAC: Only the good things, not the bad, please.

JENNY: Oh well, I see a narrow dark place and not much light. And then I see a big T, that means a woman's treachery. And then I see . . .

MAC: Stop. I'd like some details about that narrow dark place and the treachery. What's this treacherous woman's name?

JENNY: All I see is it begins with a J.

MAC: Then you've got it wrong. It begins with a P.

JENNY: Mac, when the Coronation bells start ringing at Westminster, you'll be in for a sticky time.

MAC: Go on! *Jake laughs uproariously.* What's the matter? *He runs over to Jake, and reads.* They've got it wrong, there were only three of them.

JAKE *laughs:* Exactly.

MAC: Nice underwear you've got there.

WHORE: From the cradle to the grave, underwear first, last and all the time.

OLD WHORE: I never wear silk. Makes gentlemen think you've got something wrong with you.

Jenny slips stealthily out the door.

SECOND WHORE *to Jenny:* Where are you going, Jenny?

JENNY: You'll see. *Goes out.*

DOLLY: But homespun underwear can put them off too.

OLD WHORE: I've had very good results with homespun underwear.

VIXEN: It makes the gentlemen feel they're at home.

MAC *to Betty:* Have you still got the black lace trimming?

BETTY: Still the black lace trimming.

MAC: What kind of lingerie do you have?

SECOND WHORE: Oh, I don't like to tell you. I can't take anybody to my room because my aunt is so crazy about men, and in doorways, you know, I just don't wear any. *Jake laughs.*

MAC: Finished?

JAKE: No, I just got to the rapes.

MAC *back to the sofa:* But where's Jenny? Ladies, long before my star rose over this city . . .

VIXEN: 'Long before my star rose over this city . . .'

MAC: . . . I lived in the most impecunious circumstances with one of you dear ladies. And though today I am Mac the Knife, my good fortune will never lead me to forget the companions of my dark days, especially Jenny, whom I loved the best of all. Now listen, please.

While Mac sings, Jenny stands to the right outside the window and beckons to Constable Smith. Then Mrs Peachum joins her. The three stand under the street lamp and watch the house.

BALLAD OF IMMORAL EARNINGS

There was a time, now very far away
When we set up together, I and she.
I'd got the brain, and she supplied the breast.
I saw her right, and she looked after me –
A way of life then, if not quite the best.
And when a client came I'd slide out of our bed
And treat him nice, and go and have a drink instead
And when he paid up I'd address him: Sir
Come any night you feel you fancy her.
That time's long past, but what would I not give
To see that whorehouse where we used to live?
Jenny appears in the door, with Smith behind her.

JENNY:
That was the time, now very far away
He was so sweet and bashed me where it hurt.

And when the cash ran out the feathers really flew
He'd up and say: I'm going to pawn your skirt.
A skirt is nicer, but no skirt will do.
Just like his cheek, he had me fairly stewing
I'd ask him straight to say what he thought he was doing
Then he'd lash out and knock me headlong down the
stairs.
I had the bruises off and on for years.

BOTH:

That time's long past, but what would I not give
To see that whorehouse where we used to live?

BOTH *together and alternating:*

That was the time, now very far away[8]

MAC:

Not that the bloody times seem to have looked up.

JENNY:

When afternoons were all I had for you

MAC:

I told you she was generally booked up.
(The night's more normal, but daytime will do.)

JENNY:

Once I was pregnant, so the doctor said.

MAC:

So we reversed positions on the bed.

JENNY:

He thought his weight would make it premature.

MAC:

But in the end we flushed it down the sewer.
That could not last, but what would I not give
To see that whorehouse where we used to live?
*Dance. Mac picks up his sword stick, she hands him his hat, he
is still dancing when Smith lays a hand on his shoulder.*

SMITH: Coming quietly?

MAC: Is there only one way out of this dump?
*Smith tries to put the handcuffs on Macheath; Mac gives him a
push in the chest and he reels back. Mac jumps out of the window.
Outside stands Mrs Peachum with constables.*

MAC *with poise, very politely:* Good afternoon, ma'am.

MRS PEACHUM: My dear Mr Macheath. My husband says the

greatest heroes in history have tripped over this humble threshold.

MAC: May I ask how your husband is doing?

MRS PEACHUM: Better, thank you. I'm so sorry, you'll have to be bidding the charming ladies goodbye now. Come, constable, escort the gentleman to his new home. *He is led away. Mrs Peachum through the window:* Ladies, if you wish to visit him, you'll invariably find him in. From now on the gentleman's address will be the Old Bailey. I knew he'd be round to see his whores. I'll settle the bill. Goodbye, ladies. *Goes out.*

JENNY: Wake up, Jake, something has happened.

JAKE *who has been too immersed in his reading to notice anything:* Where's Mac?

JENNY: The rozzers were here.

JAKE: Good God! And me just reading, reading, reading . . . Well, I never! *Goes out.*

6

Betrayed by the wnores, Macheath is freed from prison by the love of yet another woman.

The cells in the Old Bailey.
A cage.

Enter Brown.

BROWN: If only my men don't catch him! Let's hope to God he's riding out beyond Highgate Heath, thinking of his Jackie. But he's so frivolous, like all great men. If they bring him in now and he looks at me with his faithful friendly eyes, I won't be able to bear it. Thank God, anyway, the moon is shining; if he is riding across the heath, at least he won't stray from the path. *Sounds backstage.* What's that? Oh, my God, they're bringing him in.

MAC *tied with heavy ropes, accompanied by six constables, enters with head erect.* Well, flatfeet, thank God we're home again. *He notices Brown who has fled to the far corner of the cell.*

BROWN *after a long pause, under the withering glance of his former friend:* Oh, Mac, it wasn't me . . . I did everything . . . don't look at me like that, Mac . . . I can't stand it . . . Your silence is killing me. *Shouts at one of the constables:* Stop tugging at that rope, you swine . . . Say something, Mac. Say something to your poor Jackie . . . A kind word in his tragic . . . *Rests his head against the wall and weeps.* He doesn't deem me worthy even of a word. *Goes out.*

MAC: That miserable Brown. The living picture of a bad conscience. And he calls himself a chief of police. It was a good idea not shouting at him. I was going to at first. But just in time it occurred to me that a deep withering stare would send much colder shivers down his spine. It worked. I looked at him and he wept bitterly. That's a trick I got from the Bible.

Enter Smith with handcuffs.

MAC: Well, Mr Warder, I suppose these are the heaviest you've got? With your kind permission I should like to apply for a more comfortable pair. *He takes out his cheque book.*

SMITH: Of course, Captain, we've got them here at every price. It all depends how much you want to spend. From one guinea to ten.

MAC: How much would none at all be?

SMITH: Fifty.

MAC *writes a cheque:* But the worst of it is that now this business with Lucy is bound to come out. If Brown hears that I've been carrying on with his daughter behind his friendly back, he'll turn into a tiger.

SMITH: You've made your bed, now lie on it.

MAC: I bet the little tart is waiting outside right now. I can see happy days between now and the execution.

　　Is this a life for one of my proud station?
　　I take it, I must frankly own, amiss.
　　From childhood up I heard with consternation:

One must live well to know what living is!
Song lighting: golden glow. The organ is lit up. Three lamps are
lowered on a pole, and the signs say:

BALLADE OF GOOD LIVING[9]

I've heard them praising single-minded spirits
Whose empty stomachs show they live for knowledge
In rat-infested shacks awash with ullage.
I'm all for culture, but there are some limits.
The simple life is fine for those it suits.
I don't find, for my part, that it attracts.
There's not a bird from here to Halifax
Would peck at such unappetising fruits.
What use is freedom? None, to judge from this.
One must live well to know what living is.

The dashing sort who cut precarious capers
And go and risk their necks just for the pleasure
Then swagger home and write it up at leisure
And flog the story to the Sunday papers –
If you could see how cold they get at night
Sullen, with chilly wife, climbing to bed
And how they dream they're going to get ahead
And see the future stretching out of sight –
Now tell me, who would choose to live like this?
One must live well to know what living is.

There's plenty that they have. I know I lack it
And ought to join their splendid isolation
But when I gave it more consideration
I told myself: my friend, that's not your racket.
Suffering ennobles, but it can depress.
The paths of glory lead but to the grave.
You once were poor and lonely, wise and brave.
You ought to try to bite off rather less.
The search for happiness boils down to this:
One must live well to know what living is.

Enter Lucy.

LUCY: You dirty dog, you – how can you look me in the face after all there's been between us?

MAC: Have you no bowels, no tenderness, my dear Lucy, seeing a husband in such circumstances?

LUCY: A husband! You monster! So you think I haven't heard about your goings-on with Miss Peachum! I could scratch your eyes out!

MAC: Seriously, Lucy, you're not fool enough to be jealous of Polly?

LUCY: You're married to her, aren't you, you beast?

MAC: Married! It's true, I go to the house, I chat with the girl. I kiss her, and now the silly jade goes about telling everyone that I'm married to her. I am ready, my dear Lucy, to give you satisfaction – if you think there is any in marriage. What can a man of honour say more? He can say nothing more.

LUCY: Oh, Mac, I only want to become an honest woman.

MAC: If you think marriage with me will . . . all right. What can a man of honour say more? He can say nothing more.
Enter Polly.

POLLY: Where is my dear husband? Oh, Mac, there you are. Why do you turn away from me? It's your Polly. It's your wife.

LUCY: Oh, you miserable villain!

POLLY: Oh, Mackie in prison! Why didn't you ride across Highgate Heath? You told me you weren't going to see those women any more. I knew what they'd do to you; but I said nothing, because I believed you. Mac, I'll stay with you till death us do part. – Not one kind word, Mac? Not one kind look? Oh, Mac, think what your Polly must be suffering to see you like this.

LUCY: Oh, the slut.

POLLY: What does this mean, Mac? Who on earth is that? You might at least tell her who I am. Please tell her I'm your wife. Aren't I your wife? Look at me. Tell me, aren't I your wife?

LUCY: You low-down sneak! Have you got two wives, you monster?

POLLY: Say something, Mac. Aren't I your wife? Haven't I done everything for you? I was innocent when I married, you know that. Why, you even put me in charge of the gang, and I've done it all the way we arranged, and Jake wants me to tell you that he . . .

MAC: If you two would kindly shut your traps for one minute I'll explain everything.

LUCY: No, I won't shut my trap, I can't bear it. It's more than flesh and blood can stand.

POLLY: Yes, my dear, naturally the wife has . . .

LUCY: The wife!!

POLLY: . . . the wife is entitled to some preference. Or at least the appearance of it, my dear. All this fuss and bother will drive the poor man mad.

LUCY: Fuss and bother, that's a good one. What have you gone and picked up now? This messy little tart! So this is your great conquest! So this is your Rose of old Soho!

Song lighting: golden glow. The organ is lit up. Three lamps are lowered on a pole and the signs say:

JEALOUSY DUET

LUCY:

Come on out, you Rose of Old Soho!
Let us see your legs, my little sweetheart!
I hear you have a lovely ankle
And I'd love to see such a complete tart.
They tell me that Mac says your behind is so provoking.

POLLY:

Did he now, did he now?

LUCY:

If what I see is true he must be joking.

POLLY:

Is he now, is he now?

LUCY:

Ho, it makes me split my sides!

POLLY:

Oh, that's how you split your side?

LUCY:

Fancy you as Mackie's bride!

POLLY:

Mackie fancies Mackie's bride.

LUCY:

Ha ha ha! Catch him sporting
With something that the cat brought in.

POLLY:

Just you watch your tongue, my dear.

LUCY:

Must I watch my tongue, my dear?

BOTH:

Mackie and I, see how we bill and coo, man
He's got no eye for any other woman.
The whole thing's an invention
You mustn't pay attention
To such a bitch's slanders.
Poppycock!

POLLY:

Oh, they call me Rose of Old Soho
And Macheath appears to find me pretty.

LUCY:

Does he now?

POLLY:

They say I have a lovely ankle
And the best proportions in the city.

LUCY:

Little whippersnapper!

POLLY:

Who's a little whippersnapper?
Mac tells me that he finds my behind is most provoking.

LUCY:

Doesn't he? Doesn't he?

POLLY:

I do not suppose that he is joking.

LUCY:

Isn't he, isn't he?

POLLY:

Ho, it makes me split my sides!

LUCY:

Oh, that's how you split your side?

POLLY:

Being Mackie's only bride!

LUCY:

Are you Mackie's only bride?

POLLY *to the audience:*

Can you really picture him sporting
With something that the cat brought in?

LUCY:

Just you watch your tongue, my dear.

POLLY:

Must I watch my tongue, my dear?

BOTH:

Mackie and I, see how we bill and coo, man
He's got no eye for any other woman.
The whole thing's an invention
You cannot pay attention
To such a bitch's slanders.
Poppycock!

MAC: All right, Lucy. Calm down. You see it's just a trick of Polly's. She wants to come between us. I'm going to be hanged and she wants to parade as my widow. Really, Polly, this isn't the moment.

POLLY: Have you the heart to disclaim me?

MAC: And have you the heart to go on about my being married? Oh, Polly, why do you have to add to my misery? *Shakes his head reproachfully:* Polly! Polly!

LUCY: It's true, Miss Peachum. You're putting yourself in a bad light. Quite apart from the fact that it's uncivilised of you to worry a gentleman in his situation!

POLLY: The most elementary rules of decency, my dear young lady, ought to teach you, it seems to me, to treat a man with a little more reserve when his wife is present.

MAC: Seriously, Polly, that's carrying a joke too far.

LUCY: And if, my dear lady, you start raising a row here in this prison, I shall be obliged to send for the screw to show you the door. I'm sorry, my dear Miss Peachum.

POLLY: Mrs, if you please! Mrs Macheath. Just let me tell you this, young lady. The airs you give yourself are most unbecoming. My duty obliges me to stay with my husband.

LUCY: What's that? What's that? Oh, she won't leave! She stands there and we throw her out and she won't leave! Must I speak more plainly?

POLLY: You – you just hold your filthy tongue, you slut, or I'll knock your block off, my dear young lady.

LUCY: You've been thrown out, you interloper! I suppose that's not clear enough. You don't understand nice manners.

POLLY: You and your nice manners! Oh, I'm forgetting my dignity! I shouldn't stoop to . . . no, I shouldn't.
She starts to bawl.

LUCY: Just look at my belly, you slut! Did I get that from out of nowhere? Haven't you eyes in your head?

POLLY: Oh! So you're in the family way! And you think that gives you rights? A fine lady like you, you shouldn't have let him in!

MAC: Polly!

POLLY *in tears:* This is really too much. Mac, you shouldn't have done that. Now I don't know what to do.
Enter Mrs Peachum.

MRS PEACHUM: I knew it. She's with her man. You little trollop, come here immediately. When they hang your man, you can hang yourself too. A fine way to treat your respectable mother, making her come and get you out of jail. And he's got two of them, what's more – the Nero!

POLLY: Leave me here, mama; you don't know . . .

MRS PEACHUM: You're coming home this minute.

LUCY: There you are, it takes your mama to tell you how to behave.

MRS PEACHUM: Get going.

POLLY: Just a second. I only have to . . . I only have to tell him something . . . Really . . . it's very important.

MRS PEACHUM *giving her a box on the ear:* Well, this is important too. Get going!

POLLY: Oh, Mac! *She is dragged away.*

MAC: Lucy, you were magnificent. Of course I felt sorry for her. That's why I couldn't treat the slut as she deserved. Just for a moment you thought there was some truth in what she said. Didn't you?

LUCY: Yes, my dear, so I did.

MAC: If there were any truth in it, her mother wouldn't have put me in this situation. Did you hear how she laid into me? A mother might treat a seducer like that, not a son-in-law.

LUCY: It makes me happy to hear you say that from the bottom of your heart. I love you so much I'd almost rather see you on the gallows than in the arms of another. Isn't that strange?

MAC: Lucy, I should like to owe you my life.

LUCY: It's wonderful the way you say that. Say it again.

MAC: Lucy, I should like to owe you my life.

LUCY: Shall I run away with you, dearest?

MAC: Well, but you see, if we run away together, it won't be easy for us to hide. As soon as they stop looking, I'll send for you post haste, you know that.

LUCY: What can I do to help you?

MAC: Bring me my hat and cane.

Lucy comes back with his hat and cane and throws them into his cage.

Lucy, the fruit of our love which you bear beneath your heart will hold us forever united.

Lucy goes out.

SMITH *enters, goes into the cell, and says to Mac:* Let's have that cane.

After a brief chase, in which Smith pursues Mac with a chair and a crow bar, Mac jumps over the bars. Constables run after him. Enter Brown.

BROWN *off:* Hey, Mac! – Mac, answer me, please. It's Jackie. Mac, please be a good boy, answer me, I can't stand it any longer. *Comes in.* Mackie! What's this? He's gone, thank God.

He sits down on the bed.

Enter Peachum.

PEACHUM *to Smith:* My name is Peachum. I've come to collect the forty pounds reward for the capture of the bandit Macheath. *Appears in front of the cage.* Excuse me! Is that Mr Macheath? *Brown is silent.* Oh. I suppose the other gentleman has gone for a stroll? I come here to visit a criminal and who do I find sitting here but Mr Brown! Tiger Brown is sitting here and his friend Macheath is not sitting here.

BROWN *groaning:* Oh, Mr Peachum, it wasn't my fault.

PEACHUM: Of course not. How could it be? You'd never have dreamt . . . considering the situation it'll land you in . . . it's out of the question, Brown.

BROWN: Mr Peachum, I'm beside myself.

PEACHUM: I believe you. Terrible, you must feel.

BROWN: Yes, it's this feeling of helplessness that ties one's hands so. Those fellows do just as they please. It's dreadful, dreadful.

PEACHUM: Wouldn't you care to lie down awhile? Just close your eyes and pretend nothing has happened. Imagine you're on a lovely green meadow with little white clouds overhead. The main thing is to forget all about those ghastly things, those that are past, and most of all, those that are still to come.

BROWN *alarmed:* What do you mean by that?

PEACHUM: I'm amazed at your fortitude. In your position I should simply collapse, crawl into bed and drink hot tea. And above all, I'd find someone to lay a soothing hand on my forehead.

BROWN: Damn it all, it's not my fault if the fellow escapes. There's not much the police can do about it.

PEACHUM: I see. There's not much the police can do about it. You don't believe we'll see Mr Macheath back here again? *Brown shrugs his shoulders.* In that case your fate will be hideously unjust. People are sure to say – they always do – that the police shouldn't have let him escape. No, I can't see that glittering Coronation procession just yet.

BROWN: What do you mean?

PEACHUM: Let me remind you of a historical incident which, though it caused a great stir at the time, in the year 1400 BC, is unknown to the public of today. On the death of the

Egyptian king Rameses II, the police captain of Nineveh, or was it Cairo, committed some minor offence against the lower classes of the population. Even at that time the consequences were terrible. As the history books tell us, the coronation procession of Semiramis, the new Queen, 'developed into a series of catastrophes thanks to the unduly active participation of the lower orders'. Historians still shudder at the cruel way Semiramis treated her police captain. I only remember dimly, but there was some talk of snakes she fed on his bosom.

BROWN: Really?

PEACHUM: The Lord be with you, Brown. *Goes out.*

BROWN: Now only the mailed fist can help. Sergeants! Report to me at the double!

Curtain. Macheath and Low-Dive Jenny step before the curtain and sing to song lighting:

SECOND THREEPENNY FINALE
WHAT KEEPS MANKIND ALIVE?

You gentlemen who think you have a mission
To purge us of the seven deadly sins
Should first sort out the basic food position
Then start your preaching: that's where it begins.
You lot, who preach restraint and watch your waist as well
Should learn for all time how the world is run:
However much you twist, whatever lies you tell
Food is the first thing. Morals follow on.
So first make sure that those who now are starving
Get proper helpings when we do the carving.
    What keeps mankind alive? The fact that millions
    Are daily tortured, stifled, punished, silenced, oppressed.
    Mankind can keep alive thanks to its brilliance
    In keeping its humanity repressed.
    For once you must try not to shirk the facts:
    Mankind is kept alive by bestial acts.

You say that girls may strip with your permission.
You draw the lines dividing art from sin.
So first sort out the basic food position
Then start your preaching: that's where we begin.
You lot, who bank on your desires and our disgust
Should learn for all time how the world is run:
Whatever lies you tell, however much you twist
Food is the first thing. Morals follow on.
So first make sure that those who now are starving
Get proper helpings when we do the carving.

> What keeps mankind alive? The fact that millions
> Are daily tortured, stifled, punished, silenced, oppressed.
> Mankind can keep alive thanks to its brilliance
> In keeping its humanity repressed.
> For once you must try not to shirk the facts:
> Mankind is kept alive by bestial acts.

ACT THREE

7

That night Peachum prepares his campaign. He plans to disrupt the Coronation procession by a demonstration of human misery.

Peachum's Outfitting Emporium for Beggars.

The beggars paint little signs with inscriptions such as 'I gave my eye for my king', etc.

PEACHUM: Gentlemen, at this moment, in our eleven branches from Drury Lane to Turnbridge, one thousand four hundred and thirty-two gentlemen are working on signs like these with a view to attending the Coronation of our Queen.

MRS PEACHUM: Get a move on! If you won't work, you can't beg. Call yourself a blind man and can't even make a proper K? That's supposed to be child's writing, anyone would think it was an old man's.

A drum rolls.

BEGGAR: That's the Coronation guard presenting arms. Little do they suspect that today, the biggest day in their military careers, they'll have us to deal with.

FILCH *enters and reports:* Mrs Peachum, there's a dozen sleepy-looking hens traipsing in. They claim there's some money due them.

Enter the whores.

JENNY: Madam . . .

MRS PEACHUM: Hm, you do look as if you'd fallen off your perches. I suppose you've come to collect the money for that Macheath of yours? Well, you'll get nothing, you understand, nothing.

JENNY: How are we to understand that, Ma'am?

MRS PEACHUM: Bursting in here in the middle of the night! Coming to a respectable house at three in the morning! With the work you do, I should think you'd want some sleep. You look like sicked-up milk.

JENNY: Then you won't give us the stipulated fee for turning in Macheath, ma'am?

MRS PEACHUM: Exactly. No thirty pieces of silver for you.

JENNY: Why not, ma'am?

MRS PEACHUM: Because your fine Mr Macheath has scattered himself to the four winds. And now, ladies, get out of my parlour.

JENNY: Well, I call that the limit. Just don't you try that on us. That's all I've got to say to you. Not on us.

MRS PEACHUM: Filch, the ladies wish to be shown the door.
Filch goes towards the ladies, Jenny pushes him away.

JENNY: I would be grateful if you would be so good as to hold your filthy tongue. If you don't, I'm likely to . . .
Enter Peachum.

PEACHUM: What's going on, you haven't given them any money, I hope? Well, ladies how about it? Is Mr Macheath in jail, or isn't he?

JENNY: Don't talk to me about Mr Macheath. You're not fit to black his boots. Last night I had to let a customer go because it made me cry into my pillow thinking how I had sold that gentleman to you. Yes, ladies, and what do you think happened this morning? Less than an hour ago, just after I had cried myself to sleep, I heard somebody whistle, and out on the street stood the very gentleman I'd been crying about, asking me to throw down the key. He wanted to lie in my arms and make me forget the wrong I had done him. Ladies, he's the last sportsman left in London. And if our friend Suky Tawdry isn't here with us now, it's because he went on from me to her to console her too.

PEACHUM *muttering to himself:* Suky Tawdry . . .

JENNY: So now you know that you're not fit to black that gentleman's boots. You miserable sneak.

PEACHUM: Filch, run to the nearest police station, tell them Mr Macheath is at Miss Suky Tawdry's place. *Filch goes out.* But ladies, what are we arguing for? The money will be paid out, that goes without saying. Celia dear, you'd do better to make the ladies some coffee instead of slanging them.

MRS PEACHUM *on her way out:* Suky Tawdry! *She sings the third stanza of the Ballad of Sexual Obsession:*

> There stands a man. The gallows loom above him.
> They've got the quicklime mixed in which to shove him.
> They've put his neck just under where the noose is
> And what's he thinking of, the idiot? Floozies.
> They've all but hanged him, yet he can't ignore that call.
> Sexual obsession has him in its thrall.
>> She's sold him down the river heart and soul
>> He's seen the dirty money in her hand
>> And bit by bit begins to understand:
>> The pit that covers him is woman's hole.
>> Then he may rant and roar and curse his ruin –
>> But soon as night falls he'll be up and doing.

PEACHUM: Get a move on, you'd all be rotting in the sewers of Turnbridge if in my sleepless nights I hadn't worked out how to squeeze a penny out of your poverty. I discovered that though the rich of this earth find no difficulty in creating misery, they can't bear to see it. Because they are weaklings and fools just like you. They may have enough to eat till the end of their days, they may be able to wax their floors with butter so that even the crumbs from their tables grow fat. But they can't look on unmoved while a man is collapsing from hunger, though of course that only applies so long as he collapses outside their own front door. *Enter Mrs Peachum with a tray full of coffee cups.*

MRS PEACHUM: You can come by the shop tomorrow and pick up your money, but only once the Coronation's over.

JENNY: Mrs Peachum, you leave me speechless.

PEACHUM: Fall in. We assemble in one hour outside Buckingham Palace. Quick march.

The beggars fall in.

FILCH *dashes in:* Cops! I didn't even get to the police station. The police are here already.

PEACHUM: Hide, gentlemen! *To Mrs Peachum:* Call the band together. Shake a leg. And if you hear me say 'harmless', do you understand, *harmless . . .*

MRS PEACHUM: Harmless? I don't understand a thing.

PEACHUM: Naturally you don't understand. Well, if I say *harmless . . . Knocking at the door.* Thank God, that's the answer, *harmless,* then you play some kind of music. Get a move on!

Mrs Peachum goes out with the beggars. The beggars, except for the girl with the sign 'A Victim of Military Tyranny', hide with their things upstage right behind the clothes rack. Enter Brown and constables.

BROWN: Here we are. And now, Mr Beggar's Friend, drastic action will be taken. Put the derbies on him, Smith. Ah, here are some of those delightful signs. *To the girl:* 'A Victim of Military Tyranny' – is that you?

PEACHUM: Good morning, Brown, good morning. Sleep well?

BROWN: Huh?

PEACHUM: Morning, Brown.

BROWN: Is he saying that to me? Does he know one of you? I don't believe I have the pleasure of your acquaintance.

PEACHUM: Really? Morning, Brown.

BROWN: Knock his hat off. *Smith does so.*

PEACHUM: Look here, Brown, since you're passing by, *passing,* I say, Brown, I may as well ask you to put a certain Macheath under lock and key, it's high time.

BROWN: The man's mad. Don't laugh, Smith. Tell me, Smith, how is it possible that such a notorious criminal should be running around loose in London?

PEACHUM: Because he's your pal, Brown.

BROWN: Who?

PEACHUM: Mac the Knife. Not me. I'm no criminal. I'm a poor man, Brown. You can't abuse me, Brown, you've got the worst hour in your life ahead of you. Care for some coffee? *To the whores:* Girls, give the chief of police a sip, that's no way to behave. Let's all be friends. We are all law-abiding people. The law was made for one thing alone, for the exploitation of those who don't understand it, or are prevented by naked misery from obeying it. And anyone who wants a crumb of this exploitation for himself must obey the law strictly.

BROWN: I see, then you believe our judges are corruptible?

PEACHUM: Not at all, sir, not at all. Our judges are absolutely incorruptible: it's more than money can do to make them give a fair verdict.

A second drum roll.

The troops are marching off to line the route. The poorest of the poor will move off in half an hour.

BROWN: That's right, Mr Peachum. In half an hour the poorest of the poor will be marched off to winter quarters in the Old Bailey. *To the constables:* All right, boys, round them all up, all the patriots you find here. *To the beggars:* Have you fellows ever heard of Tiger Brown? Tonight, Peachum, I've hit on the solution, and I believe I may say, saved a friend from mortal peril. I'll simply smoke out your whole nest. And lock up the lot of you for – hm, for what? For begging on the street. You seem to have intimated your intention of embarrassing me and the Queen with these beggars. I shall simply arrest the beggars. Think about it.

PEACHUM: Excellent, but . . . what beggars?

BROWN: These cripples here. Smith, we're taking these patriots along with us.

PEACHUM: I can save you from a hasty step; you can thank the Lord, Brown, that you came to me. You see, Brown, you can arrest these few, they're harmless, *harmless* . . .

Music starts up, playing a few measures of the 'Song of the In-sufficiency of Human Endeavour'.

BROWN: What's that?

PEACHUM: Music. They're playing as well as they can. The Song of Insufficiency. You don't know it? Think about it.

Song lighting: golden glow. The organ is lit up. Three lamps are lowered from above on a pole and the signs say:

SONG OF THE INSUFFICIENCY OF HUMAN ENDEAVOUR

Mankind lives by its head
Its head won't see it through
Inspect your own. What lives off that?
At most a louse or two.
    For this bleak existence
    Man is never sharp enough.
    Hence his weak resistance
    To its tricks and bluff.

Aye, make yourself a plan
They need you at the top!
Then make yourself a second plan
Then let the whole thing drop.
    For this bleak existence
    Man is never bad enough
    Though his sheer persistence
    Can be lovely stuff.

Aye, race for happiness
But don't you race too fast.
When all start chasing happiness
Happiness comes in last.
    For this bleak existence
    Man is never undemanding enough.
    All his loud insistence
    Is a load of guff.

PEACHUM: Your plan, Brown, was brilliant but hardly realistic. All you can arrest in this place is a few young fellows celebrating their Queen's Coronation by arranging a little fancy dress party. When the real paupers come along – there aren't any here – there will be thousands of them. That's the point: you've forgotten what an immense number of poor people there are. When you see them standing outside the Abbey, it won't be a festive sight. You see, they don't look good. Do you know what grogblossom is, Brown? Yes, but how about a hundred and twenty noses all flushed with grogblossom? Our young Queen's path should be strewn with blossom, not with grogblossom. And all those cripples at the church door. That's something one wishes to avoid, Brown. You'll probably say the police can handle us poor folk. You don't believe that yourself. How will it look if six hundred poor cripples have to be clubbed down at the Coronation? It will look bad. It will look disgusting. Nauseating. I feel faint at the thought of it, Brown. A small chair, if you please.

BROWN *to Smith:* That's a threat. See here, you, that's black-mail. We can't touch the man, in the interests of public order we simply can't touch him. I've never seen the like of it.

PEACHUM: You're seeing it now. Let me tell you something. You can behave as you please to the Queen of England. But you can't tread on the toes of the poorest man in England, or you'll be brought down, Mr Brown.

BROWN: So you're asking me to arrest Mac the Knife? Arrest him? That's easy to say. You have to find a man before you can arrest him.

PEACHUM: If you say that, I can't contradict you. So I'll find your man for you; we'll see if there's any morality left. Jenny, where is Mr Macheath at this moment?

JENNY: 21 Oxford Street, at Suky Tawdry's.

BROWN: Smith, go at once to Suky Tawdry's place at 21 Oxford Street, arrest Macheath and take him to the Old Bailey. In the meantime, I must put on my gala uniform. On this day of all days I must wear my gala uniform.

PEACHUM: Brown, if he's not on the gallows by six o'clock . . .

BROWN: Oh, Mac, it was not to be. *Goes out with constables.*

PEACHUM *calling after him:* Think about it, eh, Brown?
Third drum roll.
Third drum roll. Change of objective. You will head for the dungeons of the Old Bailey.
The beggars go out.

Peachum sings the fourth stanza of the 'Song of Human Insufficiency':

> Man could be good instead
> So slug him on the head
> If you can slug him good and hard
> He may stay good and dead.
>> For this bleak existence
>> Man's not good enough just yet.
>> You'll need no assistance.
>> Slug him on the head.

Curtain. Jenny steps before the curtain with a hurdy-gurdy and sings the

SOLOMON SONG

> You saw sagacious Solomon
> You know what came of him.
> To him complexities seemed plain.
> He cursed the hour that gave birth to him
> And saw that everything was vain.
> How great and wise was Solomon!
> But now that time is getting late
> The world can see what followed on.
> It's wisdom that had brought him to this state –
> How fortunate the man with none!

> You saw the lovely Cleopatra
> You know what she became.
> Two emperors slaved to serve her lust.
> She whored herself to death and fame
> Then rotted down and turned to dust.
> How beautiful was Babylon!
> But now that time is getting late
> The world can see what followed on.
> It's beauty that had brought her to this state –
> How fortunate the girl with none!

You saw the gallant Caesar next
You know what he became.
They deified him in his life
Then had him murdered just the same.
And as they raised the fatal knife
How loud he cried 'You too, my son!'
But now that time is getting late
The world can see what followed on.
It's courage that had brought him to this state –
How fortunate the man with none!

You know the ever-curious Brecht
Whose songs you liked to hum.
He asked, too often for your peace
Where rich men get their riches from.
So then you drove him overseas.
How curious was my mother's son!
But now that time is getting late
The world can see what followed on.
Inquisitiveness brought him to this state –
How fortunate the man with none!

And now look at this man Macheath
The sands are running out.
If only he'd known where to stop
And stuck to crimes he knew all about
He surely would have reached the top.
But one fine day his heart was won.
So now that time is getting late
The world can see what followed on.
His sexual urges brought him to this state –
How fortunate the man with none!

8

Property in dispute.[10]

A young girl's room in the Old Bailey.

Lucy.

SMITH *enters:* Miss, Mrs Polly Macheath wishes to speak with you.

LUCY: Mrs Macheath? Show her in.

Enter Polly.

POLLY: Good morning, madam. Madam, good morning.

LUCY: What is it, please?

POLLY: Do you recognise me?

LUCY: Of course I know you.

POLLY: I've come to beg your pardon for the way I behaved yesterday.

LUCY: Very interesting.

POLLY: I have no excuse to offer for my behaviour, madam, but my misfortunes.

LUCY: I see.

POLLY: Madam, you must forgive me. I was stung by Mr Macheath's behaviour. He really should not have put us in such a situation, and you can tell him so when you see him.

LUCY: I . . . I . . . shan't be seeing him.

POLLY: Of course you will see him.

LUCY: I shall not see him.

POLLY: Forgive me.

LUCY: But he's very fond of you.

POLLY: Oh no, you're the only one he loves. I'm sure of that.

LUCY: Very kind of you.

POLLY: But, madam, a man is always afraid of a woman who loves him too much. And then he's bound to neglect and avoid her. I could see at a glance that he is more devoted to you than I could ever have guessed.

LUCY: Do you mean that sincerely?

POLLY: Of course, certainly, very sincerely, madam. Do believe me.

LUCY: Dear Miss Polly, both of us have loved him too much.

POLLY: Perhaps. *Pause.* And now, madam, I want to tell you how it all came about. Ten days ago I met Mr Macheath for the first time at the Cuttlefish Hotel. My mother was there too. Five days later, about the day before yesterday, we were married. Yesterday I found out that he was wanted by the police for a variety of crimes. And today I don't know what's going to happen. So you see, madam, twelve days ago I couldn't have imagined ever losing my heart to a man. *Pause.*

LUCY: I understand, Miss Peachum.

POLLY: Mrs Macheath.

LUCY: Mrs Macheath.

POLLY: To tell the truth, I've been thinking about this man a good deal in the last few hours. It's not so simple. Because you see, Miss, I really can't help envying you for the way he behaved to you the other day. When I left him, only because my mother made me, he didn't show the slightest sign of regret. Maybe he has no heart and nothing but a stone in his breast. What do you think, Lucy?

LUCY: Well, my dear Miss, I really don't know if Mr Macheath is entirely to blame. You should have stuck to your own class of people, dear Miss.

POLLY: Mrs Macheath.

LUCY: Mrs Macheath.

POLLY: That's quite true – or at least, as my father always advised me, I should have kept everything on a strict business footing.

LUCY: Definitely.

POLLY *weeping:* But he's my only possession in all the world.

LUCY: My dear, such a misfortune can befall the most intelligent woman. But after all, you are his wife on paper. That should be a comfort to you. Poor child, I can't bear to see you so depressed. Won't you have a little something?

POLLY: What?

LUCY: Something to eat.

POLLY: Oh yes, please, a little something to eat. *Lucy goes out.*
Polly aside: The hypocritical strumpet.

LUCY *comes back with coffee and cake:* Here. This ought to do it.

POLLY: You really have gone to too much trouble, madam.
Pause. She eats. What a lovely picture of him you've got.
When did he bring it?

LUCY: Bring it?

POLLY *innocently:* I mean when did he bring it up here to you?

LUCY: He didn't bring it.

POLLY: Did he give it to you right here in this room?

LUCY: He never was in this room.

POLLY: I see. But there wouldn't have been any harm in that.
The paths of fate are so dreadfully crisscrossed.

LUCY: Must you keep talking such nonsense? You only came
here to spy.

POLLY: Then you know where he is?

LUCY: Me? Don't you know?

POLLY: Tell me this minute where he is.

LUCY: I have no idea.

POLLY: So you don't know where he is. Word of honour?

LUCY: No, I don't know. Hm, and you don't either?

POLLY: No. This is terrible. *Polly laughs and Lucy weeps.* Now
he has two commitments. And he's gone.

LUCY: I can't stand it any more. Oh, Polly, it's so dreadful.

POLLY *gaily:* I'm so happy to have found such a good friend
at the end of this tragedy. That's something. Would you
care for a little more to eat? Some more cake?

LUCY: Just a bit! Oh, Polly, don't be so good to me. Really,
I don't deserve it. Oh, Polly, men aren't worth it.

POLLY: Of course men aren't worth it, but what else can we
do?

LUCY: No! Now I'm going to make a clean breast of it. Will
you be very cross with me, Polly?

POLLY: About what?

LUCY: It's not real!

POLLY: What?

LUCY: This here! *She indicates her belly.* And all for that crook!

POLLY *laughs:* Oh, that's magnificent! Is it a cushion? Oh, you
really are a hypocritical strumpet! Look – you want

Mackie? I'll make you a present of him. If you find him you can keep him. *Voices and steps are heard in the corridor.* What's that?

LUCY *at the window:* Mackie! They've caught him once more.

POLLY *collapses:* This is the end.

Enter Mrs Peachum.

MRS PEACHUM: Ha, Polly, so this is where I find you. You must change your things, your husband is being hanged. I've brought your widow's weeds. *Polly changes into the widow's dress.* You'll be a lovely widow. But you'll have to cheer up a little.

9

Friday morning. 5 am. Mac the Knife, who has been with the whores again, has again been betrayed by whores. He is about to be hanged.

Death cell.

The bells of Westminster ring. Constables bring Macheath shackled into the cell.

SMITH: Bring him in here. Those are the bells of Westminster. Stand up straight, I'm not asking you why you look so worn out. I'd say you were ashamed. *To the constables:* When the bells of Westminster ring for the third time, that will be at six, he's got to have been hanged. Make everything ready.

A CONSTABLE: For the last quarter of an hour all the streets around Newgate have been so jammed with people of all classes you can't get through.

SMITH: Strange! Then they already know?

CONSTABLE: If this goes on, the whole of London will know in another quarter of an hour. All the people who would otherwise have gone to the Coronation will come here. And the Queen will be riding through empty streets.

SMITH: All the more reason for us to move fast. If we're through by six, that will give people time to get back to the Coronation by seven. So now, get going.

MAC: Hey, Smith, what time is it?

SMITH: Haven't you got eyes? Five oh-four.

MAC: Five oh-four.

Just as Smith is locking the cell door from outside, Brown enters.

BROWN, *his back to the cell, to Smith:* Is he in there?

SMITH: You want to see him?

BROWN: No, no, no, for God's sake. I'll leave it all to you. *Goes out.*

MAC *suddenly bursts into a soft unbroken flow of speech:* All right, Smith, I won't say a word, not a word about bribery, never fear. I know all about it. If you let yourself be bribed, you'd have to leave the country for a start. You certainly would. You'd need enough to live on for the rest of your life. A thousand pounds, eh? Don't say anything! In twenty minutes I'll tell you whether you can have your thousand pounds by noon. I'm not saying a word about feelings. Go outside and think it over carefully. Life is short and money is scarce. And I don't even know yet if I can raise any. But if anyone wants to see me, let them in.

SMITH *slowly:* That's a lot of nonsense, Mr Macheath. *Goes out.*

MAC *sings softly and very fast the 'Call from the Grave':*

Hark to the voice that's calling you to weep.
Macheath lies here, not under open sky
Not under treetops, no, but good and deep.
Fate struck him down in outraged majesty.
God grant his dying words may reach a friend.
The thickest walls encompass him about.
Is none of you concerned to know his fate?
Once he is gone the bottles can come out
But do stand by him while it's not too late.
D'you want his punishment to have no end?[11]

Matthew and Jake appear in the corridor. They are on their way to see Macheath. Smith stops them.

SMITH: Well, son. You look like a soused herring.

MATTHEW: Now the captain's gone it's my job to put our girls in pod, so they can throw themselves on the mercy of

the court. It's a job for a horse. I've got to see the Captain.
Both continue towards Mac.

MAC: Five twenty-five. You took your time.

JAKE: Yes, but, you see, we had to . . .[12]

MAC: You see, you see. I'm being hanged, man! But I've no
time to waste arguing with you. Five twenty-eight. All
right: How much can you people draw from your savings
account right away?

MATTHEW: From our . . . at five o'clock in the morning?

JAKE: Has it really come to this?

MAC: Can you manage four hundred pounds?

JAKE: But what about us? That's all there is.

MAC: Who's being hanged, you or me?

MATTHEW *excitedly:* Who was lying around with Suky
Tawdry instead of clearing out? Who was lying around
with Suky Tawdry, us or you?

MAC: Shut your trap. I'll soon be lying somewhere other than
with that slut. Five-thirty.

JAKE: Matt, if that's how it is, we'll just have to do it.

SMITH: Mr Brown wishes to know what you'd like for your
. . . repast.

MAC: Don't bother me. *To Matthew:* Well, will you or won't
you? *To Smith:* Asparagus.

MATTHEW: Don't you shout at me. I won't have it.

MAC: I'm not shouting at you. It's only that . . . well,
Matthew, are you going to let me be hanged?

MATTHEW: Of course I'm not going to let you be hanged.
Who said I was? But that's the lot. Four hundred pounds is
all there is. No reason why I shouldn't say that, is there?

MAC: Five thirty-eight.

JAKE: We'll have to run, Matthew, or it'll be no good.

MATTHEW: If we can only get through. There's such a crowd.
Human scum! *Both go out.*

MAC: If you're not here by five to six, you'll never see me
again. *Shouts:* You'll never see me again . . .

SMITH: They've gone. Well, how about it? *Makes a gesture of
counting money.*

MAC: Four hundred. *Smith goes out shrugging his shoulders. Mac,
calling after him:* I've got to speak to Brown.

SMITH *comes back with constables:* Got the soap?

CONSTABLE: Yes, but not the right kind.

SMITH: You can set the thing up in ten minutes.

CONSTABLE: But the trap doesn't work.

SMITH: It's got to work. The bells have gone a second time.

CONSTABLE: What a shambles!

MAC *sings:*

Come here and see the shitty state he's in.
This really is what people mean by bust.
You who set up the dirty cash you win
As just about the only god you'll trust
Don't stand and watch him slipping round the bend!
Go to the Queen and say that her subjects need her
Go in a group and tell her of his trouble
Like pigs all following behind their leader.
Say that his teeth are wearing down to rubble.
D'you want his punishment to have no end?

SMITH: I can't possibly let you in. You're only number sixteen. Wait your turn.

POLLY: What do you mean, number sixteen? Don't be a bureaucrat. I'm his wife. I've got to see him.

SMITH: Not more than five minutes, then.

POLLY: Five minutes! That's perfectly ridiculous. Five minutes! How's a lady to say all she's got to say? It's not so simple. This is goodbye forever. There's an exceptional amount of things for man and wife to talk about at such a moment . . . where is he?

SMITH: What, can't you see him?

POLLY: Oh yes, of course. Thank you.

MAC: Polly!

POLLY: Yes, Mackie, here I am.

MAC: Oh yes, of course!

POLLY: How are you? Are you quite worn out? It's hard.

MAC: But what are you going to do now? What will become of you?

POLLY: Don't worry, the business is doing very well. That's the least part of it. Are you very nervous, Mackie? . . . By the way, what was your father? There's so much you still haven't told me. I just don't understand. Your health has always been excellent.

MAC: Polly, can't you help me to get out?

POLLY: Oh yes, of course.

MAC: With money, of course. I've arranged with the warder . . .

POLLY *slowly:* The money has gone off to Manchester.

MAC: And you have got none on you?

POLLY: No, I have got nothing on me. But you know, Mackie, I could talk to somebody, for instance . . . I might even ask the Queen in person. *She breaks down.* Oh, Mackie!

SMITH *pulling Polly away:* Well, have you raised those thousand pounds?

POLLY: All the best, Mackie, look after yourself, and don't forget me! *Goes out.*

Smith and a constable bring in a table with a dish of asparagus on it.

SMITH: Is the asparagus tender?

CONSTABLE: Yes. *Goes out.*

BROWN *appears and goes up to Smith:* Smith, what does he want me for? It's good you didn't take the table in earlier. We'll take it right in with us, to show him how we feel about him. *They enter the cell with the table. Smith goes out. Pause.* Hello, Mac. Here's your asparagus. Won't you have some?

MAC: Don't you bother, Mr Brown. There are others to show me the last honours.[13]

BROWN: Oh, Mackie!

MAC: Would you have the goodness to produce your accounts? You don't mind if I eat in the meantime, after all it is my last meal. *He eats.*

BROWN: I hope you enjoy it. Oh, Mac, you're turning the knife in the wound.

MAC: The accounts, sir, if you please, the accounts. No sentimentality.

BROWN *with a sigh takes a small notebook from his pocket:* I've got them right here, Mac. The accounts for the past six months.

MAC *bitingly:* Oh, so all you came for was to get your money before it's too late.

BROWN: You know that isn't so . . .

MAC: Don't worry, sir, nobody's going to cheat you. What do

I owe you? But I want a detailed bill, if you don't mind. Life has made me distrustful . . . in your position you should be able to understand that.

BROWN: Mac, when you talk that way I just can't think.

A loud pounding is heard rear.

SMITH *off*: All right, that'll hold.

MAC: The accounts, Brown.

BROWN: Very well, if you insist. Well, first of all the rewards for murderers arrested thanks to you or your men. The Treasury paid you a total of . . .

MAC: Three instances at forty pounds a piece, that makes a hundred and twenty pounds. One quarter for you comes to thirty pounds, so that's what we owe you.

BROWN: Yes . . . yes . . . but really, Mac, I don't think we ought to spend our last . . .

MAC: Kindly stop snivelling. Thirty pounds. And for the job in Dover eight pounds.

BROWN: Why only eight pounds, there was . . .

MAC: Do you believe me or don't you believe me? Your share in the transactions of the last six months comes to thirty-eight pounds.

BROWN *wailing*: For a whole lifetime . . . I could read . . .

BOTH: Your every thought in your eyes.

MAC: Three years in India – John was all present and Jim was all there – five years in London, and this is the thanks I get. *Indicating how he will look when hanged.*

Here hangs Macheath who never wronged a flea
A faithless friend has brought him to this pass.
And as he dangles from the gallowstree
His neck finds out how heavy is his arse.

BROWN: If that's the way you feel about it, Mac . . . The man who impugns my honour, impugns me. *Runs furiously out of the cage.*

MAC: Your honour . . .

BROWN: Yes, my honour. Time to begin, Smith! Let them in! *To Mac:* Excuse me, would you?

SMITH *quickly to Macheath:* I can still get you out of here, in another minute I won't be able to. Have you got the money?

MAC: Yes, as soon as the boys get back.

SMITH: There's no sign of them. The deal is off.

People are admitted. Peachum, Mrs Peachum, Polly, Lucy, the whores, the parson, Matthew and Jake.

JENNY: They weren't anxious to let us in. But I said to them: If you don't get those pisspots you call heads out of my way, you'll hear from Low-Dive Jenny.

PEACHUM: I am his father-in-law. I beg your pardon, which of the present company is Mr Macheath?

MAC *introduces himself:* I'm Macheath.

PEACHUM *walks past the cage, and like all who follow him stations himself to the right of it:* Fate, Mr Macheath, has decreed that though I don't know you, you should be my son-in-law. The occasion of this first meeting between us is a very sad one. Mr Macheath, you once had white kid gloves, a cane with an ivory handle, and a scar on your neck, and you frequented the Cuttlefish Hotel. All that is left is your scar, no doubt the least valuable of your distinguishing marks. Today you frequent nothing but prison cells, and within the foreseeable future no place at all . . .

Polly passes the cage in tears and stations herself to the right.

MAC: What a pretty dress you're wearing.

Matthew and Jake pass the cage and station themselves on the right.

MATTHEW: We couldn't get through because of the terrible crush. We ran so hard I was afraid Jake was going to have a stroke. If you don't believe us . . .

MAC: What do my men say? Have they got good places?

MATTHEW: You see, Captain, we thought you'd understand. You see, a Coronation doesn't happen every day. They've got to make some money while there's a chance. They send you their best wishes.

JAKE: Their very best wishes.

MRS PEACHUM *steps up to the cage, stations herself on the right:* Mr Macheath, who would have expected this a week ago when we were dancing at a little hop at the Cuttlefish Hotel.

MAC: A little hop.

MRS PEACHUM: But the ways of destiny are cruel here below.

BROWN *at the rear to the parson:* And to think that I stood shoulder to shoulder with this man in Azerbaidjan under a hail of bullets.

JENNY *approaches the cage:* We Drury Lane girls are frantic. Nobody's gone to the Coronation. Everybody wants to see you. *Stations herself on the right.*

MAC: To see me.

SMITH: All right. Let's go. Six o'clock. *Lets him out of the cage.*

MAC: We mustn't keep anybody waiting. Ladies and gentlemen. You see before you a declining representative of a declining social group. We lower middle-class artisans who toil with our humble jemmies on small shopkeepers' cash registers are being swallowed up by big corporations backed by the banks. What's a jemmy compared with a share certificate? What's breaking into a bank compared with founding a bank? What's murdering a man compared with employing a man? Fellow citizens, I hereby take my leave of you. I thank you for coming. Some of you were very close to me. That Jenny should have turned me in amazes me greatly. It is proof positive that the world never changes. A concatenation of several unfortunate circumstances has brought about my fall. So be it – I fall.

Song lighting: golden glow. The organ is lit up. Three lamps are lowered on a pole, and the signs say:

BALLAD IN WHICH MACHEATH BEGS ALL MEN FOR FORGIVENESS

You fellow men who live on after us
Pray do not think you have to judge us harshly
And when you see us hoisted up and trussed
Don't laugh like fools behind your big moustaches
Or curse at us. It's true that we came crashing
But do not judge our downfall like the courts.
Not all of us can discipline our thoughts –
Dear fellows, your extravagance needs slashing.
Dear fellows, we've shown how a crash begins.
Pray then to God that He forgive my sins.

The rain washes away and purifies.
Let it wash down the flesh we catered for
And we who saw so much, and wanted more –
The crows will come and peck away our eyes.
Perhaps ambition used too sharp a goad
It drove us to these heights from which we swing
Hacked at by greedy starlings on the wing
Like horses' droppings on a country road.
O brothers, learn from us how it begins
And pray to God that He forgive our sins.

The girls who flaunt their breasts as bait there
To catch some sucker who will love them
The youths who slyly stand and wait there
To grab their sinful earnings off them
The crooks, the tarts, the tarts' protectors
The models and the mannequins
The psychopaths, the unfrocked rectors
I pray that they forgive my sins.

Not so those filthy police employees
Who day by day would bait my anger
Devise new troubles to annoy me
And chuck me crusts to stop my hunger.
I'd call on God to come and choke them
And yet my need for respite wins:
I realise that it might provoke them
So pray that they forgive my sins.

Someone must take a huge iron crowbar
And stave their ugly faces in
All I ask is to know it's over
Praying that they forgive my sins.

SMITH: If you don't mind, Mr Macheath.
MRS PEACHUM: Polly and Lucy, stand by your husband in his last hour.
MAC: Ladies, whatever there may have been between us . . .
SMITH *leads him away:* Get a move on!

Procession to the Gallows.
All go out through doors left. These doors are on projection screens.
Then all re-enter from the other side of the stage with dark lan-
terns. When Macheath is standing at the top of the gallows steps
Peachum speaks.

Dear audience, we now are coming to
The point where we must hang him by the neck
Because it is the Christian thing to do
Proving that men must pay for what they take.

But as we want to keep our fingers clean
And you're the people we can't risk offending
We thought we'd better do without this scene
And substitute instead a different ending.

Since this is opera, not life, you'll see
Justice give way before humanity.
So now, to stop our story in its course
Enter the royal official on his horse.

THIRD THREEPENNY FINALE
APPEARANCE OF THE DEUS EX MACHINA

CHORUS:

Hark, who's here?
A royal official on horseback's here!
Enter Brown on horseback as deus ex machina.

BROWN: I bring a special order from our beloved Queen to
have Captain Macheath set at liberty forthwith – *All cheer.* –
as it's the coronation, and raised to the hereditary peerage.
Cheers. The castle of Marmarel, likewise a pension of ten
thousand pounds, to be his in usufruct until his death. To
any bridal couples present Her Majesty bids me to convey
her gracious good wishes.

MAC:
Reprieved! Reprieved! I was sure of it.
When you're most despairing
The clouds may be clearing

POLLY: Reprieved, my dearest Macheath is reprieved. I am so happy.

MRS PEACHUM: So it all turned out nicely in the end. How nice and easy everything would be if you could always reckon with saviours on horseback.

PEACHUM: Now please remain all standing in your places, and join in the hymn of the poorest of the poor, whose most arduous lot you have put on stage here today. In real life the fates they meet can only be grim. Saviours on horseback are seldom met with in practice. And the man who's kicked about must kick back. Which all means that injustice should be spared from persecution.

All come forward, singing to the organ:

Injustice should be spared from persecution:
Soon it will freeze to death, for it is cold.
Think of the blizzards and the black confusion
Which in this vale of tears we must behold.

The bells of Westminster are heard ringing for the third time.

Additional texts

Notes by Brecht

ON *The Threepenny Opera*

Under the title *The Beggar's Opera*, *The Threepenny Opera* has been performed for the past two hundred years in theatres throughout England. It gives us an introduction to the life of London's criminal districts, Soho and Whitechapel, which are still the refuge of the poorest and least easily understood strata of English society just as they were two centuries ago.

Mr Jonathan Peachum has an ingenious way of capitalising on human misery by artificially equipping healthy individuals as cripples and sending them out to beg, thereby earning his profits from the compassion of the well-to-do. This activity in no sense results from inborn wickedness. 'My position in the world is one of self-defence' is Peachum's principle, and this stimulates him to the greatest decisiveness in all his dealings. He has but one serious adversary in the London criminal community, a gentlemanly young man called Macheath, whom the girls find divine. Macheath has abducted Peachum's daughter Polly and married her in highly eccentric fashion in a stable. On learning of his daughter's marriage – which offends him more on social grounds than on moral ones – Peachum launches an all-out war against Macheath and his gang of rogues; and it is the vicissitudes of this war that form the content of *The Threepenny Opera*. However, it ends with Macheath being saved literally from the gallows, and a grand, if somewhat parodistic operatic finale satisfactorily rounds it all off.

The Beggar's Opera was first performed in 1728 at the Lincoln's Inn Theatre. Contrary to what a number of German translators have supposed, its title does not signify an opera featuring beggars but 'the beggar's opera', in other words an opera for beggars. Written in response to a suggestion by the great Jonathan Swift, *The Beggar's Opera* was a parody of Handel, and it is said to have had a splendid result in that Handel's theatre became ruined. Since there is nowadays no target for parody on the scale of Handel's theatre all attempt at parody has been abandoned: the musical score is entirely modern. We still, however, have the same *sociological* situation. Just like two hundred years ago we have a social order in which virtually all levels, albeit in a wide variety of ways, pay respect to moral principles not by leading a moral life but by living off morality. Where its form is concerned, the *Threepenny Opera* represents a basic type of opera. It contains elements of opera and elements of the drama.

['Über die Dreigroschenoper – 1' from GW *Schriften zum Theater* p.987. Dated 9 January 1929, when it appeared as an article in the *Augsburger Neueste Nachrichten* to introduce the production in Brecht's home town.]

NOTES TO *The Threepenny Opera*

The reading of plays

There is no reason why John Gay's motto for his *Beggar's Opera* – nos haec novimus esse nihil* – should be changed for *The Threepenny Opera*. Its publication represents little more than the prompt-book of a play wholly surrendered to theatres, and thus is directed at the expert rather than at the consumer. This doesn't mean that the conversion of the maximum number of readers or spectators into experts is not thoroughly desirable; indeed it is under way.

The Threepenny Opera is concerned with bourgeois conceptions not only as content, by representing them, but also through the manner in which it does so. It is a kind of report on life as any member of the audience would like to see it. Since at the same time, however, he sees a good deal that he has no wish to see; since therefore he sees his wishes not merely fulfilled but also criticised (sees himself not as the subject but as the object), he is theoretically in a position to appoint a new function for the theatre. But the theatre itself resists any alteration of its function, and so it seems desirable that the spectator should read plays whose aim is not merely to be performed in the theatre but to change it: out of mistrust of the theatre. Today we see the theatre being given absolute priority over the actual plays. The theatre apparatus's priority is a priority of means of production. This apparatus resists all conversion to other purposes, by taking any play which it encounters and immediately changing it so that it no longer represents a foreign body within the apparatus – except at those points where it neutralises itself. The necessity to stage the new drama

* 'We know these things to be nothing.'

correctly – which matters more for the theatre's sake than for the drama's – is modified by the fact that the theatre can stage anything: it theatres it all down. Of course this priority has economic reasons.

The principal characters

The character of JONATHAN PEACHUM is not to be resumed in the stereotyped formula 'miser'. He has no regard for money. Mistrusting as he does anything that might inspire hope, he sees money as just one more wholly ineffective weapon of defence. Certainly he is a rascal, a theatrical rascal of the old school. His crime lies in his conception of the world. Though it is a conception worthy in its ghastliness of standing alongside the achievements of any of the other great criminals, in making a commodity of human misery he is merely following the trend of the times. To give a practical example, when Peachum takes Filch's money in scene 1 he does not think of locking it in a cashbox but merely shoves it in his pocket: neither this nor any other money is going to save him. It is pure conscientiousness on his part, and a proof of his general despondency, if he does not just throw it away: he cannot throw away the least trifle. His attitude to a million shillings would be exactly the same. In his view neither his money (or all the money in the world) nor his head (or all the heads in the world) will see him through. And this is the reason why he never works but just wanders round his shop with his hat on his head and his hands in his pockets, checking that nothing is going astray. No truly worried man ever works. It is not meanness on his part if he has his Bible chained to his desk because he is scared someone might steal it. He never looks at his son-in-law before he has got him on the gallows, since no conceivable personal values of any kind could influence him to adopt a different approach to a man who deprives him of his daughter. Mac the Knife's other crimes only concern him in so far as they provide a means of getting rid of him. As for Peachum's daughter, she is like the Bible, just a potential aid. This is not so much repellent as disturbing, once you consider what depths of desperation are implied when nothing in the world is of any use except that minute portion which could help to save a drowning man.

The actress playing POLLY PEACHUM should study the foregoing description of Mr Peachum. She is his daughter.

The bandit MACHEATH must be played as a bourgeois phenomenon. The bourgeoisie's fascination with bandits rests on a misconception: that a bandit is not a bourgeois. This misconception is the child of another misconception: that a bourgeois is not a bandit. Does this mean that they are identical? No: occasionally a bandit is not a coward. The qualification 'peaceable' normally attributed to the bourgeois by our theatre is here achieved by Macheath's dislike, as a good businessman, of the shedding of blood except where strictly necessary – for the sake of the business. This reduction of bloodshed to a minimum, this economising, is a business principle; at a pinch Mr Macheath can wield an exceptionally agile blade. He is aware what is due to his legend: a certain romantic aura can further the economies in question if enough care is taken to spread it around. He is punctilious in ensuring that all hazardous, or at any rate bloodcurdling actions by his subordinates get ascribed to himself, and is just as reluctant as any professor to see his assistants put their name to a job. He impresses women less as a handsome man than as a well situated one. There are English drawings of *The Beggar's Opera* which show a short, stocky man of about forty with a head like a radish, a bit bald but not lacking dignity. He is emphatically staid, is without the least sense of humour, while his solid qualities can be gauged from the fact that he thinks more of exploiting his employees than of robbing strangers. With the forces of law and order he is on good terms; his common sense tells him that his own security is closely bound up with that of society. To Mr Macheath the kind of affront to public order with which Peachum menaces the police would be profoundly disturbing. Certainly his relations with the ladies of Turnbridge strike him as demanding justification, but this justification is adequately provided by the special nature of his business. Occasionally he has made use of their purely business relationship to cheer himself up, as any bachelor is entitled to do in moderation; but what he appreciates about this more private aspect is the fact that his regular and pedantically punctual visits to a certain Turnbridge coffee-house are *habits*, whose cultivation and proliferation is perhaps the main objective of his correspondingly bourgeois life.

In any case the actor playing Macheath must definitely not base his interpretation of the part on his frequenting of a disorderly house. It is one of the not uncommon but none the less incomprehensible instances of bourgeois demonism.

As for Macheath's true sexual needs, he naturally would rather satisfy them where he can get certain domestic comforts thrown in, in other words with women who are not entirely without means. He sees his marriage as an insurance for his business. However slight his regard for it, his profession necessitates a temporary absence from the capital, and his subordinates are highly unreliable. When he pictures his future he never for one moment sees himself on the gallows, just quietly fishing the stream on a property of his own.

BROWN the police commissioner is a very modern phenomenon. He is a twofold personality: his private and official natures differ completely. He lives not in spite of this fission but through it. And along with him the whole of society is living through its fission. As a private individual he would never dream of lending himself to what he considers his duty as an official. As a private individual he would not (and must not) hurt a fly. . . . In short, his affection for Macheath is entirely genuine; the fact that it brings certain business advantages does not render it suspect; too bad that life is always throwing mud at everything. . . .

Hints for actors

As for the communication of this material, the spectator must not be made to adopt the empathetic approach. There must be a process of exchange between spectator and actor, with the latter at bottom addressing himself directly to the spectator despite all the strangeness and detachment. The actor then has to tell the spectator more about his character 'than lies in the part'. He must naturally adopt the attitude which allows the episode to develop easily. At the same time he must also set up relationships with episodes other than those of the story, not just be the story's servant. In a love scene with Macheath, for instance, Polly is not only Macheath's beloved but also Peachum's daughter. Her relations with the spectator must embrace her criticisms of the accepted notions concerning bandits' women and shopkeepers' daughters.

1.* [p. 13] The actors should refrain from depicting these bandits as a collection of those depressing individuals with red neckerchiefs who frequent places of entertainment and with whom no decent person would drink a glass of beer. They are naturally sedate persons, some of them portly and all without exception good mixers when off duty.

2. [p. 13] This is where the actors can demonstrate the practical use of bourgeois virtues and the close relationship between dishonesty and sentiment.

3. [p. 14] It must be made clear how violently energetic a man needs to

* These figures refer to numbered passages in our text.

be if he is to create a situation in which a worthier attitude (that of a bridegroom) is possible.

4. [p. 17] What has to be shown here is the displaying of the bride, her fleshliness, at the moment of its final apportionment. At the very instant when supply must cease, demand has once again to be stimulated to its peak. The bride is desired all round; the bridegroom then sets the pace. It is, in other words, a thoroughly theatrical event. At the same time it has to be shown that the bride is hardly eating. How often one sees the daintiest creatures wolfing down entire chickens and fishes! Not so brides.

5. [p. 29] In showing such matters as Peachum's business the actors do not need to bother too much about the normal *development of the plot*. It is, however, important that they should present a development rather than an ambience. The actor playing one of the beggars should aim to show the selection of an appropriately effective wooden leg (trying on one, laying it aside, trying another, then going back to the first) in such a way that people decide to see the play a second time at the right moment to catch this turn; nor is there anything to prevent the theatre featuring it on the screens in the background.

6. [p. 37] It is absolutely essential that the spectator should see Miss Polly Peachum as a virtuous and agreeable girl. Having given evidence of her uncalculating love in the second scene, she now demonstrates that practical-mindedness which saves it from being mere ordinary frivolity.

7. [p. 41] These ladies are in undisturbed possession of their means of production. Just for this reason they must give no impression that they are free. Democracy for them does not represent the same freedom as it does for those whose means of production can be taken away from them.

8. [p. 44] This is where those Macheaths who seem least inhibited from portraying his death agony commonly baulk at singing the third verse. They would obviously not reject the sexual theme if a tragedy had been made of it. But in our day and age sexual themes undoubtedly belong in the realm of comedy; for sex life and social life conflict, and the resulting contradiction is comic because it can only be resolved historically, i.e. under a different social order. So the actor must be able to put across a ballad like this in a comic way. It is very important how sexual life is represented on stage, if only because a certain primitive materialism always enters into it. The artificiality and transitoriness of all social superstructures becomes visible.

9. [p. 47] Like other ballades in *The Threepenny Opera* this one contains a few lines from François Villon in the German version by K. L. Ammer. The actor will find that it pays to read Ammer's translation, as it shows the differences between a ballade to be sung and a ballade to be read.

10. [p. 66] This scene is an optional one designed for those Pollys who have a gift for comedy.

11. [p. 70] As he paces round his cell the actor playing Macheath can at this point recapitulate all the ways of walking which he has so far shown the audience. The seducer's insolent way, the hunted man's nervous way, the arrogant way, the experienced way and so on. In the course of this brief stroll he can once again show every attitude adopted by Macheath in the course of these few days.

12. [p. 71] This is where the actor of the epic theatre is careful not to let his efforts to stress Macheath's fear of death and make it dominate the whole message of the Act, lead him to throw away the depiction of *true* friendship which follows. (True friendship is only true if it is kept within limits. The moral victory scored by Macheath's two truest friends is barely diminished by these two gentlemen's subsequent moral defeat, when they are not quick *enough* to hand over their means of existence in order to save their friend.)

13. [p. 73] Perhaps the actor can find some way of showing the following: Macheath quite rightly feels that in his case there has been a gruesome miscarriage of justice. And true enough, if justice were to lead to the victimisation of any more bandits than it does at present it would lose what little reputation it has.

About the singing of the songs

When an actor sings he undergoes a change of function. Nothing is more revolting than when the actor pretends not to notice that he has left the level of plain speech and started to sing. The three levels – plain speech, heightened speech and singing – must always remain distinct, and in no case should heightened speech represent an intensification of plain speech, or singing of heightened speech. In no case therefore should singing take place where words are prevented by excess of feeling. The actor must not only sing but show a man singing. His aim is not so much to bring out the emotional content of his song (has one the right to offer others a dish that one has already eaten oneself?) but to show gestures that are so to speak the habits and usage of the body. To this end he would be best advised not to use the actual words of the text when rehearsing, but common everyday phrases which express the same thing in the crude language of ordinary life. As for the melody, he must not follow it blindly: there is a kind of speaking-against-the-music which can have strong effects, the results of a stubborn, incorruptible sobriety which is independent of music and rhythm. If he drops into the melody it must be an event; the actor can emphasise it by plainly showing the pleasure which the melody gives him. It helps the actor if the musicians are visible during his performance and also if he is allowed to make visible preparation for it (by straightening a chair perhaps or making himself up, etc.). Particularly in the songs it is important that 'he who is showing should himself be shown'.

Why does the mounted messenger have to be mounted?

The Threepenny Opera provides a picture of bourgeois society, not just of 'elements of the Lumpenproletariat'. This society has in turn produced a bourgeois structure of the world, and thereby a specific view of the world without which it could scarcely hope to survive. There is no avoiding the sudden appearance of the Royal Mounted Messenger if the bourgeoisie is to see its own world depicted. Nor has Mr Peachum any other concern in exploiting society's bad conscience for gain. Workers in the theatre should reflect just why it is so particularly stupid to deprive the messenger of his *mount*, as nearly every modernistic director of the play has done. After all, if a judicial murder is to be shown, there is surely no better way of paying due tribute to the theatre's rôle in bourgeois society than to have the journalist who establishes the murdered man's innocence towed into court by a swan. Is it not a piece of self-evident tactlessness if people persuade the audience to laugh at itself by making something comic of the mounted messenger's sudden appearance? Depriving bourgeois literature of the sudden appearance of some form of mounted messenger would reduce it to a mere depiction of conditions. The mounted messenger guarantees you a truly undisturbed appreciation of even the most intolerable conditions, so it is a *sine qua non* for a literature whose *sine qua non* is that it leads nowhere.

It goes without saying that the third finale must be played with total seriousness and utter dignity.

['Anmerkungen zur "Dreigroschenoper"', from GW *Schriften zum Theater* p.991 and *Stücke* p.992, omitting paragraphs 2

('Titles and screens') and 6 ('Why does Macheath have to be arrested twice over?'), which refer to Brecht's theatre as a whole rather than to this particular play. For these see *Brecht on Theatre*.]

Stage design for The Threepenny Opera

In *The Threepenny Opera* the more different the set's appearance as between acting and songs, the better its design. For the Berlin production (1928) a great fairground organ was placed at the back of the stage, with steps on which the jazz band was lodged, together with coloured lamps that lit up when the orchestra was playing. Right and left of the organ were two big screens for the projection of Neher's drawings, framed in red satin. Each time there was a song its title was projected on them in big letters, and lights were lowered from the grid. So as to achieve the right blend of patina and newness, shabbiness and opulence, the curtain was a small, none too clean piece of calico running on metal wires. For the Paris production (1937) opulence and patina took over. There was a real satin drapery with gold fringes, above and to the side of which were suspended big fairground lamps which were lit during the songs. The curtain had two figures of beggars painted on it, more than life size, who pointed to the title 'The Threepenny Opera'. Screens with further painted figures of beggars were placed downstage right and left.

Peachum's beggars' outfitting shop

Peachum's shop must be so equipped that the audience is able to grasp the nature of this curious concern. The Paris production had two shop windows in the background containing dummies in beggars' outfits. Inside the shop was a stand from which garments and special headgear were suspended, all marked with white labels and numbers. A small low rack contained a few worn-out shoes, numbered like the garments, of a kind only seen in museums under glass. The Kamerny Theatre in Moscow showed Mr Peachum's clients entering the dressing booths as normal human beings, then leaving them as horrible wrecks.

['Aufbau der "Dreigroschenoper"-Bühne', from GW *Schriften zum Theater* p.1000. Dated *c.* 1937. Taïroff's production at the Kamerny Theatre in Moscow took place in 1930. The Paris designer was Eugène Berman.]

Note by Kurt Weill

Thank you for your letter. I will be glad to say something about the course on which Brecht and I have embarked with this work, and which we mean to pursue further.

You speak of *The Threepenny Opera*'s sociological significance. True enough, the success of our play has shown this new gesture not merely to have come at the right moment in terms of the artistic situation but also, apparently, to have responded to a positive longing on the public's part to see a favourite form of theatre revitalised. I doubt whether our form is going to replace operetta [. . .]. What really matters to all of us is the establishment of a first bridgehead in a consumer industry hitherto reserved for a very different category of writer and musician. *The Threepenny Opera* is putting us in touch with an audience which was previously ignorant of us, or at least would never have believed us capable of interesting a circle of listeners so much wider than the normal concert- and opera-going public.

Seen thus, *The Threepenny Opera* takes its place in a movement which today embraces nearly all the younger musicians. The abandonment of 'art for art's sake', the reaction against individualism in art, the ideas for film music, the link with the musical youth movement and, connecting with these, the simplification of musical means of expression – they are all stages along the same road.

Only opera remains stuck in its 'splendid isolation'. Its audiences continue to represent a distinct group of people seemingly outside the ordinary theatrical audience. Even today new operas incorporate a dramaturgical approach, a use of language, a choice of themes such as would be quite inconceivable in the modern theatre. And one is always hearing 'That's all very well for the theatre but it wouldn't do in opera.' Opera originated as an aristocratic branch of art, and everything labelled 'operatic tradition' goes to underline its basic social character. Nowadays, however, there is no other artistic form whose attitude is so undisguisedly social, the theatre in particular having switched conclusively to a line that can better be termed socially formative. If the operatic framework cannot stand such a comparison with the theatre of the times [*Zeittheater*], then that framework had better be broken up.

Seen in this light, nearly all the worthwhile operatic experiments of recent years emerge as basically destructive in character. *The Threepenny Opera* made it possible to start rebuilding, since it allowed us to go back to scratch. What we were setting out to create was the earliest form of opera. Every musical work for the stage raises the question: what on earth can music, and particularly singing, be doing in the theatre? In our case the answer was of the most primitive possible kind. I had before me a realistic plot, and this forced me to make the music work against it if I was to prevent it from making a realistic impact. Accordingly the plot was either interrupted, making way for music, or else deliberately brought to a point where there was no alternative but to sing. Furthermore it was a play that allowed us for once to take 'opera' as subject-matter for an evening in the theatre. At the outset the audience was told 'Tonight you are going to see an opera for beggars. Because this opera was so opulently conceived as only a beggar's imagination could make it, it is called *The Threepenny Opera*.' And so even the finale to the third Act is in no sense a parody, rather an instance of the very idea of 'opera' being used to resolve a conflict, i.e. being given a function in establishing the plot, and consequently having to be presented in its purest and most authentic form.

This return to a primitive operatic form entailed a drastic simplification of musical language. It meant writing a kind of music that would be singable by actors, in other words by musical amateurs. But if at first this looked like being a handicap, in time it proved immensely enriching. Nothing but the introduction of approachable, catchy tunes made possible *The Threepenny Opera's* real achievement: the creation of a new type of musical theatre.

['Über die Dreigroschenoper' from Kurt Weill: *Ausgewählte Schriften*, ed. David Drew, Suhrkamp, Frankfurt 1975, p. 54. Originally published in *Anbruch*, Vienna, January 1929, Jg. 11, Nr. 1, p. 24, where Weill was responding to a letter from the editors welcoming the success of a work which so accurately reflected contemporary social and artistic conditions, and asking for his theoretical views.]

Conversation between Brecht and Strehler

From a conversation between Brecht and Giorgio Strehler on 25 October 1955 with regard to the forthcoming Milan production. (Taken down by Hans-Joachim Bunge.)

Strehler had prepared twenty-seven precisely formulated questions for Brecht about the production of *The Threepenny Opera*. He began by asking its relation to the original *Beggar's Opera* and the extent of Elisabeth Hauptmann's and Kurt Weill's collaboration.

Brecht and Hauptmann told him that a play had been needed to open the Theater am Schiffbauerdamm under Fischer and Aufricht's direction on 28 August 1928. Brecht was engaged on *The Threepenny Opera*. It was based on a translation made by Elisabeth Hauptmann. The ensuing work with Weill and Elisabeth Hauptmann was a true collaboration and proceeded step by step. Erich Engel agreed to take over the direction. He had directed Brecht's early plays and Brecht had attended many of his rehearsals; he was the best man for an experiment like this. Perhaps the hardest thing was choosing the actors. Brecht went primarily for cabaret and revue performers, who had the advantage of being artistically interested and socially aggressive. During the summer Caspar Neher prepared his designs. According to Brecht the idea underlying *The Threepenny Opera* was: 'criminals are bourgeois: are bourgeois criminals?'.

Strehler asked whether there was any material about the first performance. He was convinced that 'Models' were useful and therefore needed it for his production. The sort of thing that would be of historical interest to him was to know the style of the production and the historical setting of the first performance. He asked if he was right in assuming that Brecht had shifted *The Threepenny Opera* to the Victorian era because of the latter's essentially bourgeois character, which meant that London rather than, say, Paris or Berlin provided the best setting. Brecht replied that from the outset he had wanted, primarily because of the shortage of time, to change the original as little as possible. Transporting it to Paris or some other city would have meant extensive changes in the portrayal of the setting, which in turn would have entailed much additional research. But even the best of principles couldn't be maintained indefinitely, and working on the play had led to the realisation that the original date could usefully be advanced a hundred years. A good deal was known about the Victorian age, which at the same time was remote enough to be judged with critical detachment, thus permitting the audience to pick out what was relevant to them. Set in that period the play would be more easily transported to Berlin than if set in that in which Gay had (of necessity) had to locate it.

Strehler observed that the music which Weill wrote in 1928 was of its own time and therefore evidently in deliberate contrast with the period of the play. Brecht said this was a gain for the theatre. The underlying thought was: beggars are poor people. They want to make a grand opera, but lack money and have to make do as best they can. How to show this? By a splendidly entertaining performance (which at the same time, of course, must lay bare the conditions prevailing at that period) and at the same time by making evident all that which failed to achieve the object intended, frequently indeed producing results actually opposed to it. For instance the beggar actors are quite unable to portray respectability (such as ought to be particularly easy in a Victorian setting), so that there are continual lapses, particularly in the songs. The grand manner at which they are aiming goes wrong, and suddenly it all turns into a dirty joke. This isn't what the beggar actors want, but the audience loves it and applauds, with the result that it all keeps slipping further into the gutter. They are alarmed by this, but all the same it works. Their plan to create a grand theatre proves impossible to realise. Because of their restricted means it only half comes off. (Here again the Victorian age gives the right picture.) In such a beggar's opera decency would be no inducement to the audience to stay in its seats; its preferences are accordingly respected. Only the finale has once again been carefully rehearsed, so that the level originally aimed at can at least be achieved here. Yet even this is a failure, for it succeeds only as parody. In short there is a perpetual effort to present something grandiose, but each time it is a fiasco. All the same a whole series of truths emerge.

Brecht gave an instance: unemployed actors trying to portray the Geneva conference. Unfortunately they have a quite wrong idea of it, and so with the best will in the world all their crocodile-like efforts to present Mr Dulles, for instance, as a Christian martyr are a failure, because they have no proper notion either of Mr Dulles or of a Christian martyr. Whatever they do is successful only in making people laugh. But to laugh is to criticise.

Strehler suggested that *The Beggar's Opera* was originally aristocratic in both form and content, a skit on Handel's operas for instance. Brecht had kept its form and its sense. All this was still valid in 1928. Capitalist society was still on its feet then, as was grand opera. Meantime there had been a war, but the problems had remained in many ways generally the same. Today however there were distinctions that must be made. Its relevance would still apply as forcefully in Italy and similar capitalist countries.

Brecht agreed. He thought the play ought to have the same power of attack in contemporary Italy as it had had at the time in Berlin.

Strehler asked how far was *The Threepenny Opera* an epic play and how epic ought the production to be.

Brecht emphasised that both considerations to a great extent applied. The socially critical stance must not be abandoned for a moment. The main prop here was the music, which kept on destroying the illusion; the latter, however, had first to be created, since an atmosphere could never be destroyed until it had been built up.

Strehler expressed regret that so many *Threepenny Opera* productions had been prettified. Not that its socially critical aspects could be entirely camouflaged, but it had remained a nice theatrical revolution which failed to get across the footlights, not unlike those lions that can be safely visited in zoos, where you are protected from attacks by iron bars. The average director made concessions to his audience, and it wasn't going to pay 2,000 lire to have filth thrown at it. The way *The Threepenny Opera* was normally performed, like an elegant Parisian opera, everybody found it 'nice'.

Brecht explained that when *The Threepenny Opera* was originally staged in Germany in 1928 it had a strong political and aesthetic impact. Among its successful results were:

1. The fact that young proletarians suddenly came to the theatre, in some cases for the first time, and then quite often came back.
2. The fact that the top stratum of the bourgeoisie was made to laugh at its own absurdity. Having once laughed at certain attitudes, it would never again be possible for these particular representatives of the bourgeoisie to adopt them.

The Threepenny Opera can still fulfil the same function in capitalist countries today so long as people understand how to provide entertainment and, at the same time, bite instead of mere cosy absurdity. The important point now being: look, beggars are being fitted out. Every beggar is a monstrosity. The audience must be appalled at its own complicity in such poverty and wretchedness.

Strehler asked if Brecht could suggest any ways of ensuring that *The Threepenny Opera* should be as artistically effective and topically relevant in 1955 as in 1928. Brecht replied that he would heighten the crooks' make-up and render it more unpleasant. The romantic songs must be sung as beautifully as possible, but the falsity of this 'attempt at a romantic island where everything in the garden is lovely' needed to be strongly underlined.

Strehler was anxious to get material about the set, but what his Milan production most needed was some suggestions about costumes, since he felt that the 1928 costumes, which so far as he knew were based wholly on the Victorian era, would no longer be of use to him. Brecht corrected him, saying that far from being Victorian the 1928 costumes had been gathered from the costumiers and were a complete mixture. He would not think of abandoning the use of rhyme as in *The Beggar's Opera*, nor, with it, the 'jazzed up Victorianism' of the Berlin production. In the Moscow production Taïroff had entirely modernised the costumes so as to conjure up the (by Moscow standards) exotic appeal of Paris fashions.

Brecht said that Strehler had the right picture: up went the curtain on a brothel, but it was an utterly bourgeois brothel. In the brothel there were whores, but there was no mystique about them, they were utterly bourgeois whores. Everything is done to make things proper and lawful.

Strehler asked how far *The Threepenny Opera* was a satire on grand opera, to which Brecht replied: only in so far as grand opera still persists, but that this had never been so important in Germany as in Italy. The starting point must always be a poor theatre trying to do its best.

Strehler asked what did Brecht think about adaptation to bring it up to date. Brecht thought such a procedure acceptable. Strehler's question sprang from the fact that it would be impossible, for instance, to stage *The Threepenny Opera* in Naples using Kurt Weill's music. However, in Milan there were parallels with the reign of Umberto I which would be brought out. To this extent Milan was comparable with London, while the popular note struck by the music would have the same reception as in Berlin. The bourgeoisie was the same. But Strehler wondered if the need to Italianise the names might not eliminate the necessary critical detachment: for 'one must bare one's teeth for the truth'.

Brecht wondered if it might not be possible to set *The Threepenny*

Opera in the Italian quarter of New York around 1900 perhaps. The music would be right too. He had not gone into the question as yet but at the moment he thought it a possible transposition. The New York Italians had brought everything, including their emotions, from back home, but it had all got commercialised. There would be a brothel, but one like at home, to which they'd go because they felt it was 'like being back at mamma's'.

Strehler took this idea further and asked if it wouldn't mean adding a prologue. Here again Brecht agreed, in so far as some explanation would be needed. It would have to be established that the New York beggar actors were a group of Italians, that it was all like in Milan but a long way off. The first skyscrapers could have been built, but the group must be wretchedly poor. All they want to do is to stage something 'like back home'.

Strehler had a suggestion for the prologue. A film of Milan could be shown, leading the actors to want to perform something recalling that city, whereupon the curtain would rise and the play begin.

Another reservation of Strehler's concerned the Italian actor's penchant for improvisation. 'You send someone off to choose a costume and he comes back with fifty.' There was also the problem of 'the epic style of portrayal'. According to Strehler it is not easy for the Italian actor to play on more than one level at a time, i.e. roughly to the effect that 'I am acting a man trying to act this character.' He asked if it was at all possible to perform Brecht's plays – e.g. *The Mother*, which he described as the 'stronghold of the epic theatre' – except in an epic manner, and where if anywhere they could be performed if one had no actors or directors who had been trained for them. 'What is the result of acting them in the wrong way?' Brecht: 'They can certainly be performed, but what emerges is normal theatre, and three-quarters of the fun is lost.'

Strehler wanted some advice about what to do with actors who knew nothing about epic theatre. He asked if it was possible to perform a Brecht play given only *one* actor familiar with the epic theatre, and he inquired about methods for teaching the epic way of acting.

Brecht told Strehler not to worry and that our own acting too was only partly epic. It always worked best in comedies, since they anyway entail a measure of alienation. The epic style of portrayal was more easily achieved there, so that it was a good idea generally to stage plays more or less as comedies. He suggested using an aid which he had tried himself: having the actors intersperse what he called 'bridge verses', thus turning their speech into a report in indirect speech; i.e. interspersing the sentences with 'said he's. 'What's bad is that "epic" cannot be achieved without using the dialectic.'

Strehler said he was convinced that nowadays it was impossible to act either Shakespeare or the earlier tragedies without alienation if their performance was to be useful and entertaining.

Brecht once again suggested acting tragic scenes for their comic effect. What is most epic, he maintained, is always the run-throughs, and they should certainly be scheduled for the end of the rehearsals or better still conducted at regular intervals throughout the whole rehearsal period. 'The nearer the performance gets to being a run-through, the more epic it will be.' Strehler asked if his way of explaining epic portrayal to his actors was the right one, when he would cite the example of a director acting a scene, showing the actors in outline how to do something and all the time having his explanations ready even if he never voices them. Brecht approved of this and thought that the actors too could be put in the director's situation if one instituted run-throughs with minimal use of gesture, so that everyone simply noted how things should go.

Strehler feared that his *Threepenny Opera* production might turn out 'neither fish nor fowl'. His sense of responsibility had held him back from doing *Mother Courage*, since he was unable to find an epic actress to play the title part. This production of *The Threepenny Opera* too was something that he had been planning for years and always had to put off because of a shortage of suitable actors.

['Über eine Neuinszenierung der Dreigroschenoper', from *Bertolt Brechts Dreigroschenbuch* (Suhrkamp, Frankfurt 1960) pp.130–4. Strehler's production for the Piccolo Teatro, Milan, in 1957 eventually transposed the play to an American setting around the time of the First World War, with the police as Keystone Cops and an early motor car on stage. Brecht and Elisabeth Hauptmann thought it excellent.

At the Geneva Conference of summer 1954 the Western powers, China and the Soviet Union agreed to create two Vietnams, North and South. John Foster Dulles was then US Secretary of State. King Umberto I's reign in Italy was from 1878 to 1900.]

Notes

1   An early version of the play was called 'The Pimp's Opera'. The title *The Threepenny Opera* was bestowed by Brecht's friend, the writer Lion Feuchtwanger, and was then adopted by Brecht and Weill. In being based on John Gay's original, it is important to note that *The Beggar's Opera* is singular, not plural. Brecht did not write an opera for beggars to perform but an opera written and staged by a beggar for the entertainment of other beggars. The irony is that the actual audience is likely to be well-off, while the apparent cheapness of the opera is really rather expensive from a beggar's point of view. During the period when *The Threepenny Opera* is set – roughly the late nineteenth century – three old pence would have bought basic foodstuffs such as bread, milk and cheese which the average beggar could ill afford even after a successful day's begging.

2   *Elisabeth Hauptmann*: translated Gay's play which then became the basis of Brecht's re-working.

Macheath: the name is borrowed from Gay where the rogue is a highwayman rather than a murderous gang leader. The name means literally 'son of the heath', places like Hampstead Heath and Highgate Heath being notorious haunts of highwaymen and footpads at one time.

Peachum: name taken from Gay where the character is a fence, i.e. a receiver of stolen goods, rather like Fagin in Dickens' *Oliver Twist*. His name comes from ''peach 'em' (i.e. 'impeach them'). In other words, he is also an informer who turns members of his thieving gang over to the police if they fail to bring in enough money.

Celia Peachum: name taken from Gay.

Polly Peachum: name taken from Gay.

Brown: not in Gay where the nearest equivalent character is the Newgate gaoler, Lockit, who has a criminal 'gentlemen's agreement' with Peachum similar to the one Brown has with Macheath.

High Sheriff of London: there is no such position. Tiger Brown is Chief of Police.

Lucy: name taken from Gay, where she is Lockit's daughter, betrothed to Macheath and already pregnant by him.

Low-Dive Jenny: adapted from Gay's 'Jenny Diver', who is also one of Macheath's whores.

Smith : not in Gay.

The Reverend Kimball: not in Gay.

Filch: a character taken from Gay whose name is slang for 'to thieve'.

Beggars: there is only one beggar in Gay who opens the play with a description of what is to come and returns in the final scene to contrive a happy ending.

3   *The Ballad of Mac the Knife*: many of the songs in the play are termed 'ballads' and owe a debt to Gay's 'ballad opera', as it was called, and also to the 'ballades' of the French medieval poet François Villon who was, rather like Baal, the eponymous hero of Brecht's first play, a libertine, brawler, thief, scholar, rake and murderer. A ballad was originally a song for dancing but by the sixteenth century described anything simple sung by a solo voice. The ballad seller of broadsides or broadsheets was popular in England up until the eighteenth century. Any murder, accident or tragedy could be made the subject of a ballad, usually opening with the words, 'Come all you tender-hearted Christians/And

listen unto me ...', not unlike the opening of Peachum's morning hymn. A ballad opera was a peculiarly English form of theatrical entertainment consisting of a spoken play with frequent songs, the music of which was borrowed from popular songs of the day. The popularity of *The Beggar's Opera* led to the composition of about 90 ballad operas between 1728 and 1736.

Soho: a region of London's West End notorious for its 'low life' and today still the site of brothels and strip-clubs. The area extends between Shaftesbury Avenue and Oxford Street and became the chief foreign quarter of London after the revocation of the Treaty of Nantes (1685) caused thousands of French Protestant refugees to flee across the channel and settle here. Soho is also noted for its numerous foreign shops and restaurants and for its cosmopolitan atmosphere.

The beggars are begging ... etc.: the play is consistently ironic at the expense of a world which is seen to be unchangeable, where social conditions restrict the development of human potential, and where people tend to be ascribed definitive, permanent attributes. A ballad-singer in the German original is a 'Moritatensänger', i.e. one who sings 'moritats', which are ballads about 'deeds of death' or sensational violence.

turbid: muddy.

plague: the last occasion when bubonic plague struck London was during the sixteenth century.

cholera: an illness, often fatal, contracted from drinking contaminated water.

the Strand: a London street running parallel to the River Thames from Waterloo Bridge to Trafalgar Square. Germans might mistake this reference for 'a beach', for which the German word is 'Strand'.

Schmul Meier: an invented Jewish name.

across the stage from left to right: stage left and stage right are from the actors' point of view, which is the reverse of the spectators'. Brecht is very specific at points where it would not seem to make much difference whether the stage is being crossed in one direction or another, unless perhaps the directions have political significance.

4 *Jenny Towler*: an invented name.

the Embankment: a broad pavement, with a flanking river wall, built in the nineteenth century which runs alongside the River Thames through most of central London and which is illuminated at night by street lamps of Victorian design positioned on the wall.

Alfred Gleet: 'Alfons Glite' in the German original. An invented name.

the ghastly fire in Soho: presumably an arson attack instigated by Mac the Knife (called 'Mackie Messer' in the German original).

Act One

5 *Peachum's Morning Hymn*: the only song in the play which retains the tune from *The Beggar's Opera,* derived from an original air, 'An old woman, clothed in grey'.

to the audience: in Brecht's notion of epic theatre the pretence that the audience isn't really there is deliberately repudiated by forms of direct address such as this, as well as the deliberate shift of theatrical tone and focus from words which are sung to words which are spoken.

6 *'It is more blessed to give than to receive'* – despite being a radical and an atheist, the Bible was among Brecht's favourite works and is frequently drawn upon in his plays. Here the reference is to Acts 20: 35.

'Give and it shall be given unto you' – Matthew 5: 42.

It's this way, Mr Peachum: this is obviously a rehearsed speech, as suggested by Peachum's seeming to know how it continues, as if genuine misery can only be theatrically 'fictitious'. The beggar has learned his lines and repeats them by rote.

Highland Street: there is no Highland Street in London.

no suspicion of anything nasty – destitution, in order to appear acceptable and non-threatening (and therefore elicit sympathy) has to be acted out and, therefore, becomes a mere spectacle with the proffered money a reward for performance. This perception of poverty as pretence is still current. A *Daily Mail* headline of 21 May 2003 ran, 'Fake Beggars on £200 a day'.

7   *then they gave me your business card*: the apparent contrast with the beating is revealed to be part and parcel of the same process. Peachum is like a Mafia boss who runs a protection racket in which violence and 'civilised' business deals go hand in hand. This suggests the connection Brecht is making between criminal and bourgeois patterns of behaviour.

practise the craft of begging: as if begging were a skilled trade, like shoemaking, practised by professionals under a legitimate licensing authority and with its own guild.

Ten bob: ten shillings, the equivalent of 50p.

Baker Street ... That comes even cheaper: a well-known street in London made famous by Arthur Conan Doyle whose Sherlock Holmes lived at 221b. The implication here may be that, because it is a fashionable area, a beggar is likely to earn less, so that the difference between fifty and seventy per cent of the take is not very significant. This indicates that a beggar earns more in poorer areas where people are more generous but is then made to part with a higher percentage of his earnings.

8   *Coronation*: Queen Victoria was crowned in 1837. This does

not coincide with the setting of the play, which seems to be roughly in the late nineteenth century.

Victim of the Higher Strategy ... attenuated by medals: in other words, a war veteran. *The Threepenny Opera*'s first performance was a mere ten years after the First World War which was still very much in people's minds at the time.

the Cordon Bleu of Beggary: the 'Blue Ribbon' or four-star beggary. The term is more usually associated with high-class cuisine. In the German original the reference is to the 'Higher School' of beggary.

outfit D: this is not described.

a gentleman doesn't put on filthy clothes?: where the word 'gentleman' occurs in the German text, Brecht usually gives the English word rather than the German 'Herr'.

9 *We all know your feet are dirty*: Filch's fastidiousness and shame about his dirty feet make him a petty-bourgeois beggar. Later, Polly, in her song on p.27 describes her attraction to men with dirty, rather than clean collars, and it is not the 'fine gentleman' aspects of Macheath that attract her but something coarser.

Celia, the way you chuck your daughter around: it is clear that Peachum sees his daughter as an investment not to be squandered on the likes of Macheath but groomed to marry into real money and class. She also attracts beggars to the business.

10 *White gloves and a cane with an ivory handle ... and a scar*: Peachum does not set eyes on Macheath until Act Three, Scene Nine, when he repeats this line in Macheath's presence. His question as to who Macheath actually *is*, is echoed in the next scene by Macheath's asking who Peachum is. The play is consistently concerned with the question of what constitutes a human being.

11 Brecht's use of signs giving the song titles is an example of

Verfremdung (see p. xxxviii).

12 *Bare stable*: ironically in fashionable parts of London, former stables were in fact later converted into expensive and desirable houses.

Matt of the Mint: a character in Gay. The Mint is where the nation's currency is coined and printed. Matt is possibly a forger, among other things.

along the footlights: footlights were placed at floor level along the front of the stage and lit the actors' faces from below. They were largely discarded during the twentieth century as their effects were considered to be too crude and melodramatic.

13 *Crook-fingered Jake*: 'Crook-fingered Jack' in Gay.

Congratulations!: the formal greetings of a bourgeois wedding are followed in each case by descriptions of the acts of violence which have been necessary for the wedding to be celebrated in style.

Bob the Saw: not in Gay.

West End: the fashionable area of London between the City and Hyde Park which distinguished itself from the East End where the poorer classes lived.

Dreary Walt: Wat Dreary in Gay.

A rosewood harpsichord along with a renaissance sofa: Mac, in a display of bourgeois sensibility, affects to be offended by the aesthetic disharmony and clash of periods. This does not prevent him from ordering that the legs be sawn off the harpsichord to form something to sit on. The harpsichord was a very fashionable instrument during the eighteenth century. A renaissance sofa would have been an elaborately carved piece of furniture from the sixteenth century or possibly earlier.

They lay some planks over the bins: an analogy between horse troughs and bourgeois feeding habits is established, continued in 'fodder' below.

14   *For once I'm having a wedding ... Shut up, Dreary!*: may imply it has, in fact, happened before.

Ned: 'Nimming Ned' in Gay. In Brecht's play he is called Ede, pronounced as in 'header'.

Whose wedding dress was this?: the rather sad attempts of poor people to live by the standards and values of their so-called betters is parodied in the song in which the married couple scarcely know each other and can only afford a second- or third-hand wedding dress. Bill Lawgen and Mary Syer are names invented by Brecht. They should perhaps be 'Logan' and 'Sawyer'.

May I now ask the gentlemen to take off those filthy rags: a reversal of the first scene in which Peachum is sorting out 'filthy rags' for his beggars to put on.

15   *Daventry*: a town in the Midlands between Northampton and Rugby.

Chippendale: very fine English furniture made by Thomas Chippendale (1718–79) and very expensive.

Louis Quatorze: furniture in the extravagant style of the reign of Louis XIV of France (1643–1715).

fashionable evening dress: white tie and tails à la Fred Astaire.

keep it up, old china: with sexual innuendo. 'China' is cockney rhyming slang. China plate = mate.

Mac, don't be so vulgar: Polly, incongruously, seems not to mind the sexual innuendo but objects to Mac's use of the word 'slut' or possibly to him causing a row.

16   *Mr Crook-finger Jake*: Polly is a stickler for the niceties of bourgeois behaviour in addressing a criminal as 'Mr'.

17   *Savoy Hotel*: built 1903–10 and situated in a courtyard off the Strand overlooking the river Thames. It is still one of London's best-known and most expensive hotels. If the

period of the play is late nineteenth century, then Brecht has got his dates wrong; not that it matters.

plover's eggs: a culinary delicacy.

Selfridge: a large department store founded in 1909 and situated on Oxford Street near Marble Arch. Again, Brecht's sense of period is slightly awry.

foie gras: an expensive pâté made from the livers of geese which have been deliberately force-fed: normally bought in small amounts.

We don't talk about holes in polite society: a perfectly innocent remark is rendered salacious by the implication that it has sexual connotations.

18 *Have you boys got the least idea what that* [a human being] *is?*: perhaps the most important question the play raises, which will be discussed and sung about by Peachum and others. Macheath clearly thinks he knows the answer. So does Peachum. Brecht asks us to be less sure.

A human being or a human pee-ing?: in the original, Walter asks, 'Der Mensch oder das Mensch?' with no play on words. The difference in German is between a masculine and a neuter noun. 'Mensch' (a human being) is masculine but refers equally to both men and women. An animal, 'Tier' in German, is neuter. The translators' 'human pee-ing' seems designed to capture the reductionist perspective which places man on a par with animals, like the notion of 'das Mensch' (neuter) rather than 'der Mensch' (masculine).

Really, Mr Walter!: in translation, it looks as if Polly is responding to the indecency of the pun. In the original she is more like a schoolmarm upbraiding a schoolboy for not knowing his grammar.

I find you in a lowly hut ...: a possibly blasphemous reference to the place of Christ's birth. The gangsters have performed the function of the Three Wise Men in bearing

gifts to a stable. The connection between Macheath and
Christ is further developed in the final scene.

A humble place but your own: the translators are
paraphrasing *As You Like It* V, iv, 36: 'An ill-favoured thing,
sir, but mine own'.

19   *Penurious!*: poverty-stricken. Macheath likes to demonstrate
the range of his vocabulary. Here he is describing the
singers' performance rather than the subjects of the song.

it's an imitation of a girl: Polly does not indulge the
emotions of the song as if she were Pirate Jenny, but acts
out Jenny's real status and feelings in an objective and
demonstrative fashion. Polly's relationship with her
immediate audience (the gang) is part of the alienation effect
with her larger audience in the theatre, designed to make
them analyse their reaction to the song.

20   *Well, when's your ship coming in, Jenny?*: when do you
think you are going to become wealthy?

22   *Two knives, Captain*: presumably, in the absence of a fork,
the Reverend Kimball is using two knives and eating off one
of them. The difference between him and Jake is that the
vicar's breach of etiquette stems from politeness (he does not
complain about the absence of a fork) and so Jake, as Mac
suggests, still has something to learn in the world of manners.

the Old Bailey: London's Central Criminal Court, built
between 1902 and 1905 on the site of the old Newgate gaol.
The Old Bailey is not a prison.

the drop: sentenced to be hanged.

Hullo, Jackie. Hullo, Mac!: Brecht economically establishes
the strength of the bonds between former comrades-in-arms
which are more powerful than their supposedly hostile
positions on different sides of the law.

Jimmy: 'Jemmy', an old-fashioned diminutive of James, in
Gay.

23   *the king's inscrutable wisdom*: as the coronation of a new
      queen concludes the play we have to assume that the king in
      question has died.

      served in India: India was an important British colony during
      the nineteenth century and Victoria was even crowned
      Empress of India. British military might retained it against all
      opposition, the suppression of which was sometimes very
      bloody. A good deal of Brecht's understanding of the British
      experience in India was gained from his reading of Rudyard
      Kipling.

      Not that the army gave a bugger who they were: Brecht's
      concern about inhuman treatment of human beings and his
      awareness of how a man can be transformed by
      circumstances. In Brecht's earlier play with a colonial theme,
      Man equals Man, he explores the question in the person of
      one Galy Gay, an Irishman, who is transformed from a
      docker into a human fighting machine.

      From the Cape to Cooch Behar: from Cape Comorin at the
      southern tip of India to Koch Behar in the Assam region of
      N.E. India, i.e. from one end of the sub-continent to the
      other; or the Cape in question may be the Cape of Good
      Hope, South Africa.

      beefsteak tartare: a dish made of raw chopped steak.

24   *boyhood friends*: this kind of camaraderie established as
      schoolboys and continuing into adult life is especially
      associated in Britain with the tradition of the public school
      and 'the old school tie'.

      Castor and Pollux: twin sons of Zeus, the foremost of the
      Greek gods, and Leda with whom he mated in the form of a
      swan.

      Hector and Andromache: a mythical hero of the Trojan War
      and his wife. There is a sexually ambiguous aspect to the

relationship between Macheath and Tiger Brown (see pp. 31, 54 etc.), with Brown taking on the woman's role at moments of high emotion.

it's all a matter of give and take. Think about it: a parody of the religious slogans in Scene One: 'It is more blessed to give than to receive' and 'Give and it shall be given unto you!' (pp.6–7).

Genuine Shiraz: an expensive Persian carpet.

25   *Scotland Yard*: London Metropolitan Police Headquarters.

our own little iron in the fire: Matt is presumably referring to the imminent revelation of the bed.

pièce de résistance: French expression meaning most important item, something superb, usually in a culinary sense.

they sing the Bill Lawgen song: note that the manner of the song's delivery differs markedly from the earlier rendering (p.19) here underlining the men's interpretation of the power of the sexual attraction between Polly and Macheath.

26   *Look at the moon over Soho*: the terms of the song which follows need to be seen in the light of Mr and Mrs Peachum's cynical interpretation of the same romantic image in 'The "No They Can't" Song' (pp.11–12).

Where'er you go I shall be with you. / And where you stay, there too shall I be.: a parody of the Book of Ruth 1:16: 'For whither thou goest, I will go; and where thou lodgest, I will lodge.' There is also an echo of the 'Wedding Song for Poor People' in line 3.

Emporium – a pompous word for a shop.

First you rig her fore and aft: to fit a ship with masts and rigging at both the front and rear of the sailing vessel. There may be an echo here of the Pirate Jenny song.

27   *IN A LITTLE SONG . . .*: In an earlier version of the play, Polly was to sing John Gay's, 'Virgins are like the fair flower in its lustre', which then became 'The Ballad of the Virgin', then

the present song.

Sure, the boat is on the river, tied up tight: this line is repeated in verses 1 and 2 and with a variation in verse 3, the key words being 'losgemacht' (repeated twice) and 'festgemacht' in the last verse. The first means 'let loose', the second 'made fast'. The present translation reverses the meanings. The original suggests that Polly is loose when saying 'No' but makes fast when she says 'Yes'.

Wapping: an area of East London's dockland and especially associated with shipping. The local reference is not in Brecht who simply refers to the second man having three ships in port ('im Hafen').

28 *And he went and hung his hat on the nail*: precisely what Macheath is described as doing when he visits the brothel later (p.41).

a horse-thief and a highwayman: this describes Gay's Macheath but not Brecht's.

at five in the afternoon: the time scheme of the play is very precise. The final scene begins just after 5 a.m. and ends shortly before 6 a.m.

29 *Cordial Médoc*: Médoc is the name of a French wine and is not a cordial taken to improve a person's health. Mrs Peachum is permanently drunk in Gay's opera.

scabies: a contagious skin disease.

30 *engagement*: the German text uses the English word. 'To extend an engagement' has theatrical connotations which Peachum's use of the words 'artist', 'perform', 'audience', and 'applaud' emphasises.

experienced stick-up man: Polly has no illusions about Mac and is untroubled about the morality of his profession. At the same time she is concerned about his savings and appears to have petty-bourgeois ambitions.

that Mr Shakespeare: surprise is often expressed at what

seems to have been the petty-bourgeois ambition of England's greatest writer – to gain a coat-of-arms for his family and retire to the countryside in Stratford-upon-Avon. *But I love him*: the love theme in the play is very important. For Brecht it seems crucial to man's humanity and he is not in the least cynical about it.

31 *When he's hanged ... widows will turn up*: the connection between marriage and death, and between sex and death is a consistent theme of the play. Mrs Peachum appears obsessed with the basically sexual nature of human relationships.
forty pounds: the sum is taken from Gay and relates to the 'Highwayman Act' of 1692 which offered a £40 reward for information leading to the arrest of a criminal.
Turnbridge: a non-existent London region. Gay refers to Tunbridge at one point, which is a town in Kent.

32 *'Where'er you go I shall be with you.'*: a sentiment which Polly and Macheath exchanged earlier (p.26), with the implication that Brown and Macheath are sentimental masculine lovers.
Mr Macheath, you once had ...: Peachum's description of Macheath is one which might appear on a police dossier. Peachum repeats it three times during the course of the play. *and within the foreseeable future no place at all ...*: that which is criminal about Peachum, according to Brecht, is 'his conception of the world' (p.82). Here, it is evident that the professing Christian has no belief in an afterlife whatsoever.
Who's Mac the Knife?: Peachum repeats Macheath's earlier question about Peachum.

33 *And have bread on his table rather than a stone*: Peachum has the Bible in his hand and is here referring to Matthew 7:9: 'Or what man is there of you, whom if his son ask bread, will he give him a stone?'

Act Two

35   *Thursday afternoon*: again the time scheme of the play is
very specific. Macheath is a creature of habit who, like a
good businessman and bourgeois, leads a very ordered life.
He always visits the brothel on Thursdays as if it were a
visit to his club.
There's nothing on record against me: a repeated refrain.
Ironically, police records are not as reliable as those of the
criminals.
You've killed ...: Macheath has not done these things
personally, of course, but as he says later (p.38), a professor
would never allow his research assistant to lay claim to his
professorial publications even if they include errors.

36   *She throws herself on his neck*: as if in anticipation of the
rope which will encircle it. This is more powerfully
suggested in Gay, 'Where is my dear husband? Was a rope
ever intended for this neck! Oh, let me throw my arms
about it, and throttle thee with love!' (Act Two, Scene
Thirteen).
Here are the ledgers: Polly's romantic concern with
Macheath's future fidelity is brusquely cut short by
Macheath's more practical concerns. Here it becomes
apparent that Macheath's role as receiver is rather like that of
Peachum in Gay's opera, as is his cynical attitude towards
those members of his gang who don't measure up.
Just turn him in to Brown: Polly's tearful echoing of
Macheath's hardheadedness reveals her willingness to learn
and later, when she starts ordering the gang around, it is still
with Macheath's voice and manner.

37   *goes stiff, stands up ... washes his hands*: Macheath behaves
both like an animal and a human. His reaction to the word
'bloodhounds' is an instinctive one, like a fox, but the act of
washing his hands is symbolic, as if trying to obliterate the

human scent which animals would follow.

Jack Poole's banking house in Manchester: a fictitious bank in a real location.

It's only a matter of weeks before I go over to banking altogether. It's safer and it's more profitable: compare with Macheath's remarks on p.76, 'What's breaking into a bank compared with founding a bank?', which emphasise the connection between normal business and criminality.

Those gaol-birds? ... Gentlemen, it's a pleasure to see you: what Brecht says about Brown on p.84 is relevant to Macheath's also having a 'twofold personality' capable of changing the way he speaks as the occasion requires.

38   *from upstage*: Macheath is like the puppet-master pulling the strings which prompt Polly's responses.

then all clap like mad: it is not that the gang like being insulted. They are applauding Polly's performance.

gilt-edged: a term originally applied to writing paper and books before being applied commercially to business deals 'edged with gold' i.e. with absolute confidence of gain and no risk of loss.

Greenwich Children's Hospital: there is a Greenwich Hospital designed by Christopher Wren and built at the end of the seventeenth century but it was never a hospital for children.

Oxford College: 'Oxford professor' in the original. The translators are attempting to imply that Macheath does not realise that there is no Oxford College as such, only a university and colleges which are part of it. Macheath is referring ironically to the professor's laying claim to his own 'mistakes', when these should of course be blamed on his assistant.

39   *We settle up every Thursday*: the gang's day for payment coincides with Mac's brothel visits.

drinking up the empties: like someone doing a tour of used glasses in a pub and drinking the dregs in each; a metaphor for consorting with undesirable, or worthless women in this case.

I'll take my black stallion: the highwayman motif is implausible in a late-nineteenth-century context but perhaps it is not to be taken literally in this romantic exchange.

Highgate Heath: an area of common land in North London which used to be the haunt of highwaymen.

all thin like a worn-down penny: a fairly meaningless conceit as a worn-down penny would still be like a full moon. The old penny was a large bronze coin about four times the size of the present 1p. The entire scene is deliberately written in romantic clichés.

Nice while it lasted: taken from the first chorus of Kipling's poem, 'Mary, pity women', but without its suggestion of cockney speech.

40   *ten shillings*: half one pound sterling, the equivalent of 50p but only available in banknote form.

THE BALLAD OF SEXUAL OBSESSION: this song was not in the original 1928 production and appeared for the first time in a Kurt Weill song-album in 1929. Mrs Peachum is echoing Peachum's credo that man is always brought low by his sexual appetites whatever his ideals might be – a cynicism which some commentators believe the play as a whole shares.

41   *shifts*: simple petticoats.

I don't think he'll ever come again: Jake echoes Polly's line on p.39.

VIXEN: Mrs Vixen in Gay. A vixen is a female fox.

Throws the warrant on the floor: the warrant for his arrest.

Anyhow, its raining: in Brecht's *Man equals Man* a military sergeant known as 'Bloody Five' responds to weather in the

manner of animals – his sexual urges being prompted by
rain.

DOLLY: Dolly Trull in *Gay*, a trull being slang for a whore.

BETTY: Betty Doxy in *Gay*. The OED describes a doxy as 'a
beggar's trull'.

42   *Westminster*: Westminster Abbey, founded by William the
Conqueror in the eleventh century, where Britain's kings and
queens have traditionally been crowned.

43   *back to the sofa*: not 'with his back turned towards the sofa'
but 'returning to the sofa and sitting'.

BALLAD OF IMMORAL EARNINGS: Brecht borrowed this number
from a ballad by François Villon, the 'Ballade de la Grosse
Margot' (Ballad for Fat Margot) courtesy of a German
translation by Karl Klammer which Brecht failed to
acknowledge. The sentimental song about a relationship
between a pimp and his whore is ironically juxtaposed with
the presence of Jenny who has betrayed her former pimp to
the police. Originally, Macheath was to sing a version of
Kipling's 'The Ladies', about a cockney soldier who gains
sexual experience from fraternising with 'the natives'.

44   *sword stick*: a walking stick, the handle of which belongs to a
sword hidden inside it. For Brecht this is the perfect symbol
of the bourgeois-criminal whose spotless kid gloves also
conceal blood-stained hands.

45   *greatest heroes in history have tripped over this humble
threshold*: the theme of Mrs Peachum's ballad about 'sexual
slavery'. She seems to be thinking of sexual indiscretions
which have been the undoing of politicians and statesmen as
well as the classic archetypes of sexual infatuation such as
Antony and Cleopatra.

rozzers: slang for 'police'.

he looks at me with his faithful friendly eyes: like the love of a dog for its master. The fact that Brown refers to the moon shining to light Macheath's flight path also retains its romantic associations, as does the sense of 'straying from the path' with its implications of infidelity.

46 *flatfeet*: a derogatory term for policemen.

That's a trick I got from the Bible: Luke 22:61–2. Following Peter's denial of Christ: 'And the Lord turned, and looked upon Peter [...] And Peter went out, and wept bitterly.'

one guinea: a guinea was a coin representing one pound one shilling, thus 50 guineas was £50 and 50 shillings (or £52 10s.0d.)

47 *Ballade*: 'The Ballade of Good Living' also owes a debt to Villon, this time to his 'Les Contrediz de Franc Gontier' (Franc Gontier Refuted).

ullage: refuse or rubbish.

Halifax: an industrial town in the north of England. The original text has 'Babylon', ancient capital of Babylonia which is now part of modern Iraq.

One must live well to know what living is: Brecht might describe this as the unwritten law of bourgeois society.

The paths of glory lead but to the grave: a line from Thomas Gray's 'Elegy Written in a Country Churchyard', which is the translators' version of 'Und Künheit ausser Ruhm auch bittre Mühe' (And courage not only fame but bitter toil).

48 *to become an honest woman*: Lucy, it seems, also has respectable bourgeois ambitions 'to be made an honest woman', legally married, although Mac is playing with the idea of whether marriage to him will make her honest. We later discover that her pregnancy is feigned, unlike her counterpart in *The Beggar's Opera*.

till death us do part: Polly is quoting from the church marriage service, although their wedding has not been consecrated by the church.

Not one kind word, Mac? Not one kind look?: Polly is more or less repeating what Tiger Brown has said to Macheath earlier (p.46).

51 *All right, Lucy*: Macheath's decision to side with Lucy is a tactical one and also serves to consolidate his own authority through a policy of 'divide and rule'. The women's lack of solidarity simply plays into his hands. At the same time, his stating that 'I'm going to be hanged and she wants to parade as my widow', has more than a grain of truth in it.

The most elementary rules of decency: despite the fact that passions are running high, the two women still feel obliged to obey laws of decorum which belong to the drawing room rather than the prison cell.

52 *I'll knock your block off, my dear young lady*: the line is comic in mixing the styles of a catfight with polite conversation.

Nero: Emperor of Rome (54–68 AD) and famous for his dissolute behaviour.

53 *I'd almost rather see you on the gallows than in the arms of another*: the subtext of the line links Lucy with Pirate Jenny as an example of exploited women who, consciously or subconsciously, seek the extermination of men.

I'll send for you post haste: i.e. by express mail.

the fruit of our love: Macheath's use of exaggerated euphemism underlines his insincerity.

After a brief chase ... with a chair and crow bar: the effect of the scene is intensified if the alienation-effect employed suggests a lion-tamer entering the cage with the lion and is played quite seriously as if real danger were involved.

55 *Rameses II*: king of Egypt, 1304–1236 BC and famous for ordering the construction of rock temples at Luxor and Abu

Simbel.

Nineveh: capital of ancient Assyria from the eighth century BC, destroyed by the Medes in 612 BC as forecast by the Old Testament prophet Nahum. It was situated in what is now Iraq.

Cairo: present-day capital of Egypt situated on the east bank of the river Nile and founded *c.*1000 AD.

Semiramis: Greek name for the legendary queen of the Assyrians, *c.*800 BC.

the mailed fist: a fist protected by armour, the use of violence.

SECOND THREEPENNY FINALE: in the German text, the parts of the song are divided between Macheath, Jenny and voices offstage. See p.lxx.

the seven deadly sins: Lust, Gluttony, Sloth, Envy, Avarice, Pride and Anger. Prudentius, a Roman of the fifth century AD, created the characters in his *Psychomachia* but they are more commonly associated with the medieval morality play.

Food is the first thing. Morals follow on: or 'Food first. Morals after.' Probably the best-known line in the play and commonly said to represent Brecht's own cynical point of view. However, the alienation effect derives from the fact that it is only when he has nothing to lose that the well-fed Macheath feels free to embrace the view that it would be more important for a starving person to acquire food by any means rather than worry about behaving in a morally correct manner. The significance of the song's meaning should not be undermined by the fact that its sentiments are in the mouths of a cynical pimp and murderer facing the gallows, and that of his former whore.

Mankind is kept alive by bestial acts: an ironic corollary of Matthew 4:4, 'Man shall not live by bread alone.'

Act Three

57   *in our eleven branches*: like a bank or a chain of retail shops,
     which lends a kind of respectability to Peachum's sordid
     trade.

     Drury Lane: a street in London's West End connecting High
     Holborn with Aldwych and with the famous Drury Lane
     Theatre near the Aldwych end.

     If you won't work, you can't beg: a possible echo of the
     Soviet slogan immediately after the 1917 revolution, 'He who
     doesn't work, doesn't eat!'

58   *No thirty pieces of silver for you*: the amount paid to Judas
     for betraying Christ.

     scattered to the four winds: on early maps of the world
     Cupid-like figures with puffed-out cheeks, representing the
     four winds, were conventionally depicted at the four corners
     of the map.

     You're not fit to black his boots: the streets of London used
     to be populated by 'shoeshine men' offering to clean the
     footwear of passers-by. The occupation was considered
     menial. Jenny is suggesting that Peachum is someone even
     lower in the social scale.

     Suky Tawdry: name taken from Gay. 'Tawdry' means cheap
     and gaudy.

59   *quicklime*: a substance thrown into graves in order to cause
     more rapid decomposition of the corpse.

     sold him down the river: betrayed. The origin of the
     expression dates from the time when American slave owners
     sold domestic slaves to plantations further down the
     Mississippi River where conditions were harsh.

     Fall in: military instruction to assemble in ordered ranks.

60   *derbies*: handcuffs.

     Knock his hat off: when the wearing of hats was common,
     raising it to a woman or a superior was a mark of courtesy

or deference. As Peachum shows no signs of making this respectful gesture, Brown chooses to enforce it.

62   SONG OF THE INSUFFICIENCY OF HUMAN ENDEAVOUR: the sentiments also relate to the 'Solomon Song'. Man is not 'sharp', 'bad' or 'undemanding' enough for this 'bleak existence' but if he had all the virtues they would bring about his downfall anyway. This song is, of course, sung by Peachum.

When the real paupers come along: Peachum is presumably not referring to 'real' paupers, but to his beggar employees who are about to enforce an embarrassing (for Brown) confrontation with the police before the eyes of officialdom and royalty.

63   *grogblossom*: blotches or pimples on the face produced by heavy drinking.

You can behave as you please ... the poorest man in England: a typically cynical sentiment from Peachum, who doesn't believe a word of it.

21 Oxford Street: an unlikely address. Suky Tawdry's address is more likely to be a narrow lane off Oxford Street.

64   *Man could be good instead / So slug him on the head*: this advice may be said to have been taken up by the likes of Hitler and Stalin. If a person is not prepared to be a good citizen of the Third Reich or a believer in the glorious communist future, then s/he must be *forced* to behave appropriately, and if that force proves to be fatal then ... so be it.

a hurdy-gurdy: not a barrel organ but a stringed musical instrument where the music is produced by the friction of a rosined wheel on the strings, which are stopped by means of keys. The whole is operated by turning a handle and was used by street or fairground musicians.

Solomon: a biblical king of Israel, son of David and

Bathsheba and noted for his wisdom, who reigned *c.*975 BC.
A variant of the 'Solomon Song' reappears in Brecht's play
Mother Courage and her Children and Solomon's famous
judgement of the chalk circle is used in his play *The
Caucasian Chalk Circle.* The song itself is indebted to
another 'ballade' by François Villon, the 'Double Ballade',
from his 'Testament'. The 'Solomon Song' refers to the Song
of Songs (or Song of Solomon) in the Old Testament, also
known as 'Canticles'.

Cleopatra: queen of Egypt from 51–30 BC, placed on the
throne by Julius Caesar, who fathered a son on her. She later
took Mark Antony as her paramour. After losing the battle
of Actium to Octavius Caesar she and Antony committed
suicide.

65 *Caesar*: Julius Caesar, Roman statesman and general and,
latterly, emperor who lived from 102–44 BC when he was
assassinated.

You too, my son!: 'Et tu Brute' (You, too, Brutus). The
words supposedly spoken by Caesar as he was stabbed by
Brutus, whom he had trusted and who he believed was not
among the conspirators plotting his downfall.

You know the ever-curious Brecht: this verse was not in the
original version but was added in 1938 – by which time, as
the verse suggests, Brecht had been driven out of Germany
by the Nazis.

66 *A young girl's room in the Old Bailey*: it is extremely
doubtful whether the Old Bailey has any young girl's rooms!
The tone of the ensuing scene is extremely complex as the
women vie with each other for possession of their respective
'property', namely Macheath. First they try to deceive each
other, then apparently abandoning this in face of a shared
predicament, they appear to be honest with one another
before, once again, resuming the conflict over the possession

of Macheath. Beneath the comedy of the scene, there is a genuine sense of the tragedy of false human and sexual relationships which their simultaneous laughing and weeping at one point underwrites.

And you can tell him so when you see him: Polly is 'fishing'. Ostensibly she has come to apologise; in fact she is trying to ascertain the nature of Macheath's relationship with Lucy and his whereabouts.

Do you mean that sincerely?: the scene plays with notions of sincerity and insincerity, disclosure and concealment.

67   *Yesterday I found out ...*: Polly is lying. She has known all along.

68   *Here. This ought to do it*: in *The Beggar's Opera* Lucy tries to poison Polly who, however, fails to drink the glass of liquor Lucy presses upon her.

Oh, you really are a hypocritical strumpet!: contrast the tone of this with the same expression, given as an *aside*, at the top of the same page.

69   *widow's weeds*: a widow's black garments.

Polly changes into the widow's dress: the manner in which this is done is important. Grief needs to be seen to be theatrically assumed as poverty was shown to be earlier, but Polly is also a sorry victim – of a process which her mother stage-manages.

Mac the Knife ... has again been betrayed: see the section of Brecht's essay entitled 'Why Does Macheath Have to be Arrested Twice Over?' from 'The Literarization of the Theatre' (Notes to *The Threepenny Opera*) in Willett, 1964, pp.45–6), where Brecht is at pains to point out that an interest in Macheath's fate needs to be diverted from the individual to the state of society. Throughout this scene, in another blasphemous analogy, Macheath becomes a Christ figure, betrayed for thirty pieces of silver, 'crucified' on a

Friday and calling on his Father in Heaven to forgive others
for not knowing what they do.

Newgate: Newgate prison, since medieval times London's
largest. It was demolished in 1902.

70   *a soft unbroken flow of speech*: perhaps a sign that, faced
with the reality of death, sheer animal fear is uppermost. The
shivering rhythm of the song which follows would tend to
stress this fact.

Hark to the voice that's calling you to weep: with a debt to
Villon's 'Epistre (à ses amis)' 'Epistle (to his friends)'.

Girls in pod ... mercy of the court: Matt is looking the
worse for wear because, as he explains, it his now his job to
get the whores pregnant so that they can plead their delicate
condition when they are arrested and come before the courts,
to obtain a lighter, more compassionate, sentence. In *The
Beggar's Opera*, the task falls to Filch and the best the girls
can hope for is transportation, i.e. being shipped to Australia.

71   *... repast*: Smith is trying to avoid the indelicacy of 'final
repast'.

Asparagus: Macheath still has the presence of mind and
bourgeois reflexes to break off from his haranguing of Matt
to order a gourmet's hors d'oeuvre.

72   *Got the soap?*: presumably this is to moisten the noose so
that it slips nicely round the condemned man's neck.

not the right kind: presumably what is required is not a
toilet requisite but something like saddle soap.

the trap: that part of the gallows on which the condemned
person stands and which is then opened by means of a lever.
If the trap fails to work on three consecutive occasions, the
condemned man is reprieved, if he hasn't already died of
fright.

What a shambles!: what a mess! The term derives from 'The
Shambles', a street in a medieval town where the butchers

plied their trade, throwing all the leftover bits of meat into the 'channel' (a central gutter) of the thoroughfare.

73   *All the best Mackie, look after yourself, and don't forget me!*: is Polly being extremely insensitive or ironic? Or is Brecht emphasising that even in this kind of situation, people can only fall back on the inadequate clichés of ordinary conversation?

the last honours: these become grotesquely confused with the priest's 'last rites' as Brown and Smith perform the role of waiters tending to Macheath's physical, rather than spiritual needs, on the brink of the grave.

the accounts: in a conventional Christian world, Macheath is about to give an account of himself before his Maker, but Macheath's priorities are financial not spiritual.

74   *A loud pounding is heard*: work on the gallows.

the Treasury: it looks as if the money to pay Macheath for informing on his accomplices (which equates him with Peachum) is being paid out of the government exchequer.

John was all present and Jim was all there: the first line of the 'Cannon Song'.

75   *you once had white kid gloves . . .*: Peachum repeats the description he supplied earlier (p.32).

76   *Azerbaidjan*: an area now divided between N.W. Iran and the former Soviet Union, whose inhabitants are Muslim (Shiah) ethnic Turks.

We Drury Lane girls: not performers at the theatre but those who ply their trade in that street.

Everybody wants to see you: an ambiguous compliment if the women prefer to see Macheath being hanged rather than watch the queen's coronation procession.

a share certificate: issued to the purchaser of 'shares' in a company, who then receives a percentage of the profits (if the company makes one) in proportion to his investment.

This is much more profitable and, Mac implies, a greater crime than stealing from a small shopkeeper.

What's breaking into a bank compared with founding a bank?: in this analogy banks are established to use other people's money for the profitability of the bank which then lends its clients' own money back to them at exorbitant rates of interest. This is a worse crime than bank robbery, which can be regarded as a means used by some clients to retrieve their own money – with interest.

What's murdering a man compared with employing a man?: it is certainly true that, in the nineteenth century, work in a mine or a factory was the equivalent of a death sentence, given the appalling conditions and the consequent shorter life expectancy of the employees.

BALLAD IN WHICH MACHEATH BEGS ALL MEN FOR FORGIVENESS: this ballad is a reworking of two of Villon's poems, 'L'Epitaph Villon (Ballade des pendus)' ('Villon's Epitaph (Ballad of the Hanged)') and his 'Ballade (de mercy)' ('Ballad (of pardon)') and generates some of the compassion for the plight of the condemned person which is there in the original.

77   *Someone must take a huge iron crowbar . . .*: as here, this quatrain is given printed emphasis in the original text. Villon's poem is not aimed specifically at upholders of law and order and runs as follows: 'Let their ribs be mauled / with good stout mallets, / with cudgels and balls of lead. / To one and all I cry for pardon.'

78   *dark lanterns*: lanterns with their shutters closed emitting a minimum of light.

deus ex machina: literally, 'a god out of the machine' (Latin). The origin of the term goes back to Greek drama in fifth-century BC. A tragedy might conclude with a pagan god being 'flown in' by a mechanical device suspended above the stage, in order to resolve the crisis and provide a resolution to the drama. See p. 87 for Brecht's notes on the mounted messenger.

The castle of Marmarel: an invented family seat.

in usufruct: a legal term meaning the enjoyment, or profitable possession of, something.

79   *this vale of tears*: the biblical 'valley of the shadow of death', which purports to describe the world in which we all live.

Brecht's Notes to *The Threepenny Opera*

Brecht's 'Notes to *The Threepenny Opera*' were written some two years after the premiere and were first published in 1931. They were written after Brecht had adopted a more committed Marxist position and was anxious to defend the play from frivolous interpretations.

81   *The reading of plays*: the epigraph to *The Beggar's Opera* which John Gay borrowed from the Latin epigrammatist Martial (Marcus Valerius Martialis, 40–104 AD) seemed designed, at the time, as a covert disclaimer of satirical intent. The fact that Brecht considers it an appropriate motto for *The Threepenny Opera* is ironic, as *The Threepenny Opera* is overtly satirical and does not seek to hide the fact. The play may seem light-hearted in terms of those formal means and methods which it adopts but, as far as the content is concerned, it is in earnest. A major interest of the play derives precisely from this contrived clash between form and content. Brecht's idea of a popular theatre was not simply 'populist' but one in which new audiences would begin to make different, and more challenging, demands of both themselves and their entertainers. He goes on to characterise what he calls the 'bourgeois' theatre as something which can convert any conceivable subject matter into an acceptable

form, even that which is most critical of its norms, in so far as it 'theatres it all down'. Brecht recognises that contemporary Western theatre is, by and large, in the hands of the bourgeoisie where even the most radical productions tend to be tailored to the tastes of paying bourgeois audiences. He was certainly aware of the danger that, after his death, his own plays could become mere grist to the bourgeois theatrical mill.

82 *The principal characters*: the most important point to note about Peachum is Brecht's statement that his crime 'lies in his conception of the world' – one which mistrusts anything 'that might inspire hope' and 'sees money as just one more wholly ineffective weapon of defence'. While he makes 'a commodity of human misery', he is merely following the trend of the times. He has no personal values and Brecht sees this as implying the depths of his desperation.

Brecht characterises Macheath as 'a bourgeois phenomenon' and further claims that the bourgeoisie hold two misconceptions: that a bandit is not a bourgeois and that a bourgeois is not a bandit. Brecht is seeking to alienate our normal view of accepted phenomena. It is rare for the cop to be depicted in a worse light than the robber. However, as is implied in the play, the real robbers are inside the bank managing it with police protection, while the robbed are ordinary members of the public outside the bank who submit to being fleeced. Those who seek to redress the situation by robbing a bank are simply placing themselves in the same moral scale as those who set up banks in order to rob the general public. The felons are punished because their actions serve to remind bourgeois society of similarities between banking and robbery. Macheath is a crook but he is also a businessman who 'sees his marriage as an insurance for his business'.

84   *Hints for actors*: Brecht's first sentence warns the spectator
      (as well as the actor) against empathising (identifying
      emotionally) with the characters on stage. Although he does
      not specifically mention the *V-effekt*, he is suggesting the
      need for critical distance between the actor and the role
      being performed which, ideally, encourages a critically
      distanced stance in the spectator. He then goes on to specify
      particular moments in the play where a director/actor needs
      to be critically aware of how a scene is prepared and acted
      out. Some of Brecht's observations are oblique and rather
      difficult, he implies, for his contemporaries to grasp. His
      'hints' appear to be aimed at theatre practitioners of the
      future. As he states under point 8, the conflicts and
      contradictions in the play 'can only be resolved historically,
      i.e. under a different social order'.

86   *About the singing of the songs*: the points to note here are
      related to effects of estrangement where the distinctions
      between acting and singing need to be sharply differentiated.
      This is in opposition to those traditional operas which
      contain spoken dialogue and where a smooth or unmarked
      transition from speech to song is the norm. Preparation for
      the transition from the one to the other is aided by the
      visibility of the musicians on stage as they perform (and are
      also seen preparing to play) rather than having them
      concealed in an orchestra pit.

87   *Why does the mounted messenger have to be mounted?*: the
      reference to the journalist being towed into court by a swan
      would seem to be a reference to some of the absurdities of
      Wagnerian grand opera which are taken perfectly seriously
      by performers and audience alike. The fact that this elaborate
      ploy is designed to establish a murdered man's innocence is,
      of course, meant to be heavily ironic – a fact made apparent
      by Brecht's reference to 'judicial murder'. What happens in

the play is that 'the swan', in the shape of the mounted messenger, arrives on stage not in order to expose the state's guilt for the capital murder of an innocent person but to save a real murderer from the public hangman. In other words, the whole thing is a stage-managed, grotesque, hypocritical charade – like bourgeois society in general Brecht would have us believe.

88 *Stage design for* The Threepenny Opera: here Brecht provides a detailed description of the setting for the first production. Note that the organ is described as a 'fairground' one rather than anything with religious connotations. A half-curtain, running on wires, a few feet back from the proscenium arch, was to become a standard feature of Brechtian 'epic' production. Behind it the stagehands would be seen clearing or preparing the stage, as well as the actors taking up their positions for the ensuing scene. The curtain also served as a screen for the projection of slogans or pictorial images.

Peachum's beggars' outfitting shop: the key term here is 'curious' with its understatement. Both the Paris and Moscow versions seemed valid to Brecht (while adopting totally contrasting methods) in finding ways to make Peachum's bizarrely outrageous occupation seem part of a generally accepted (and acceptable) state of affairs where 'the normal' and 'the horrible' amounted to one and the same thing.

Questions for Further Study

How are relationships between Macheath, Polly, Lucy, and Jenny represented in the play?

How is the triangular relationship between Macheath, Peachum, and Tiger Brown represented in the play?

How does *The Threepenny Opera* portray relations between the sexes?

To what extent is *The Threepenny Opera* too entertaining to be taken seriously?

There are cynical characters in *The Threepenny Opera* but is the overall mood of the work one of cynicism?

How do 'alienation' effects function in the play and how might these be made to work in a production?

How are the themes of money and poverty handled in *The Threepenny Opera*?

The Threepenny Opera targets what it calls 'bourgeois society'. What do you understand by the term and how is this society characterised in the play?

How far and in what ways does *The Threepenny Opera* explore the notion of what it means to be 'human'?

How is the Christian religion represented in *The Threepenny Opera*?

Given limited resources, how would you consider staging *The*

Threepenny Opera to greatest effect for a predominantly youthful audience?

How do *The Beggar's Opera* and *The Threepenny Opera* differ as works of political satire?

'The play's political significance is overrated; its truly revolutionary effect lies in its assault on the whole hierarchical order of the arts.' To what extent would you agree?

A play with music, or an opera with dialogue? Where should the emphasis fall in *The Threepenny Opera* and why?

Hostile reviews of the first production of *The Threepenny Opera* spoke of 'literary necrophilia' and of a 'political horror ballad', as well as describing it as a 'noxious cesspool'. Which aspects of the play do you think gave rise to these reactions and why?

Discuss the relationship between the 'romantic' and the 'real' in *The Threepenny Opera*.

What is the specific effect gained from the combination of Weill's music and Brecht's words?

Brecht updated the eighteenth century to the late nineteenth century; Giorgio Strehler updated his production from the late nineteenth century to the early twentieth century. How best might a production of *The Threepenny Opera* be updated to the early twenty-first century?

Brecht's brand of 'epic' theatre sought to distinguish itself from Stanislavsky's brand of 'psychological' theatre in dealing with 'types' rather than 'characters' and in 'presentation' rather than 'identification'. Explore whether a Stanislavskian approach to *The Threepenny Opera* might be valid.

Brecht's critique of capitalist society in *The Threepenny Opera* was made from the position of someone who espoused the communist faith and opposed the rise of fascism. How far does the 'defeat' of Nazism and the 'collapse' of Soviet communism detract from the relevance of the play?